N

MYTHS THAT CAUSE CRIME

Myths that
cause crime

Harold E. Pepinsky
Paul Jesilow

Seven Locks Press
Cabin John, Md./Washington, D.C.

Copyright©Harold E. Pepinsky and Paul Jesilow

Library of Congress Cataloging in Publication Data

Pepinsky, Harold E.
    Myths that cause crime.

    Bibliography: p.
    Includes index.
    1. Crime and criminals—United States. 2. Criminal
justice, Administration of—United States.
I. Jesilow, Paul, 1950-   . II. Title.
HV6789.P46 1984   364'.973   84-14085
ISBN 0-932020-35-6

Manufactured in the United States of America

Typography and composition by Options Type Group,
Takoma Park, Maryland

Printed by the Maple Press Company, York, Pennsylvania

First edition, September 1984

Seven Locks Press
Publishers
7425 MacArthur Boulevard
P.O. Box 72
Cabin John, Maryland 20818
301-320-2130

Seven Locks Press is an affiliate of Calvin Kytle Associates

To Rosalie, Ted, and Katy

HAROLD E. PEPINSKY and PAUL JESILOW are both on the faculty in the department of forensic studies at Indiana University in Bloomington. ¶ Dr. Pepinsky was born in Lawrence, Kansas, and holds an A.B. (with distinction in Chinese language and literature) from the University of Michigan, a J.D. from Harvard Law School, and a Ph.D. from the University of Pennsylvania. ¶ Dr. Jesilow grew up in a Mexican-American neighborhood in Los Angeles. He attributes much of his interest in criminology, especially in white-collar crime, to the inequities he saw there. A sociologist and political scientist, he is a graduate of the University of California at Irvine. ¶ This is their first collaboration.

FOREWORD
by Gilbert Geis

FIRST-RATE INTELLECTUAL WORK requires fresh and iconoclastic thought. Otherwise, it is apt to become prey to the technicians, who vie with each other in attempts to do the same thing, only better. They never question the endeavor itself, never ask whether in truth they are tackling the most important problems or, indeed, whether they are examining a problem that is of any importance at all. Their single-minded aim is to accomplish the task with consumate skill, and to awe their fellows who might have done the same work less satisfactorily.

Occasionally, though, scholars will stand aside from the passing parade and begin to ask fundamental questions: Are the suppositions that guide the research themselves supportable? Is the received wisdom of the field merely folklore entrenched by years of repetition? Whose interests are served by what propositions and are those interests necessarily commensurate with the well-being of the entire society? What, after all, is going on here? Where does truth lie?

This book offers such a refreshingly close scrutiny of what has long been regarded as a common base of com-

Gilbert Geis is a past president of the American Society of Criminology and a professor in the program of social ecology at the University of California, Irvine.

mon sense knowledge. It finds that scrupulous review of the facts and careful analysis of the assumptions lead to conclusions other than those that have persisted overly long as explanations for criminal behavior and for the treatment of those who are apprehended and processed for having committed such behavior. We learn, for instance, that drug addiction was not always a crime, and that the laws that declared it to be illegal undoubtedly have created more misery than they have accomplished good. Addicts are condemned to death by statutes that force them to employ unsterilized needles and to inject contaminated drugs. To support a drug habit, they are forced to steal and to become involved in other criminal acts that can be as dangerous for them as they can be for their victims. "Treatment" will be harshly punitive rather than understanding and caring; readdiction seems the inevitable consequence of imprisonment and drying out. In short, the drug laws are a mess, maintained in place by the myth that they seek to help drug users when in truth they needlessly harm them.

Similar myths pervade the practice of criminal justice, and in this book Harold Pepinsky and Paul Jesilow root some important ones out and expose them to a cleansing light. The authors hark back to a basic principle: the law should seek to protect all of us from harm and deprivation. Therefore, it ought to be determined with scrupulous care what things are harmful and how such dangers might be remediable. If greater injury is inflicted by impure air, automobiles built with known safety inadequacies, unnecessary medical surgery, and by similar kinds of white-collar activity than by street offenses, then we would be well advised to expend the greater portion of our enforcement effort and remediation skills in an attempt to bring such social ills under better control. This idea seems so obvious that it is a wonder that it has not been acknowledged by all specialists examining the subject of crime. But it typically is ignored, bypassed as a rather embarrassing and inconvenient example of logic in a field that sometimes seems to be dedicated to pursuing and refining the illogical. Street crime is absorbing drama; suite crime is too complicated, perhaps too close-to-home to command sustained attention. Who wants the tough task of fighting power when such titillating fashions in crime concern as child sexual abuse can be used to arouse emotions and preoccupy remedial talents and resources? Child abuse is a serious problem, of course, but this book by Pepinsky and Jesilow demands that we get our priorities in better order and determine whether it is indeed more serious, and whether it should consume more social energy than, say, restrictive drug laws or toxic waste disposal issues.

Myths That Cause Crime is an optimistic book, perhaps unduly so. Harold E. Pepinsky is an ardent follower of Chinese social and political customs, a scholar with a law degree and a sociology doctorate. Paul Jesilow was trained in a multidisciplinary department. Together, the authors possess an unusual ability to see things on a broader scope than most of us, with our more confined academic indoctrinations. For these two, the hope for the future does not lie in Marxist or free-enterprise cliches and panaceas, but rather in social rearrangements which give wider range for human propensities for accommodation. They believe that people are basically good. This may be an illusion, or it may represent no more than a semantic conclusion—people obviously behave both well and poorly and it is difficult to say which is their "natural" predilection. But the idea that people truly are fundamentally good, unless corrupted by their surroundings, is a convenient and pleasant position, and it may in fact bring out a certain goodness that otherwise would not become manifest. All of us have a tendency to act in a manner that others convey that they expect of us. Pepinsky and Jesilow maintain, therefore, that a decent social system ought to decrease formal and wasteful adversarial court processes, which are largely directed against the powerless and disadvantaged, and institute mediation arrangements which would allow human beings to come together to work out their differences. This may be a Utopian position, but it assuredly seems superior to a continued policy of unthinking and discriminatory vengeance directed against those who happen to be most vulnerable to our slings and arrows.

There is some very good and sharp writing in this treatise as well as sound thought. I particularly liked the analogy between the operation of magnets, and our attempts to maximize simultaneously swiftness, sureness, and certainty of punishment. This and similarly clean analysis have a way of bringing home the points crisply.

I would emphasize, in conclusion, that crime of all sorts can be meaningfully reduced. Of that there is no question. Compare, if you will, the stunning difference between the rates of law violation by women and men not only in the United States but in all western societies. The same cultural imperatives and similar family constellations fail to elicit criminal behaviors of nearly the same quantity for males as contrasted to females. And some societies have strikingly different crime rates than others: the difference between Japan and the United States, two highly industrialized societies, is illustrative. At the same time, Japan and Sweden, rather similar in may respects, have shown astonishingly different outcomes in the results of their efforts to deal with an amphetamine abuse problem they shared in the 1950s. Japan brought its problem under control; Sweden is still grappling with a high rate of usage. Perhaps neither country took the best approach;

but the point is that different kinds of people in different places and different ways of dealing with such people can produce significantly different results. In this regard, *Myths That Cause Crime* represents a clarion call to open up a debate that is far too long overdue. Myths may be reassuring and comforting at times, but those we hold about crime have proven self-defeating: this volume should serve to strip away many of our preconceptions about crime and its treatment, and make us all better for having jettisoned inappropriate intellectual baggage.

June, 1984

CONTENTS

Author's Preface

THE TRADITIONAL ideas about crime and the proper role of criminal justice were never summed up better than in President Ronald Reagan's 1981 speech to the International Association of Chiefs of Police:

In dealing with crime, new programs may be justified, the studies and surveys may still be needed, the blue ribbon panels may keep investigating; but, in the end, the war on crime will only be won when an attitude of mind and a change of heart takes place in America, when certain truths take hold again and plant their roots deep into our national consciousness.

Truths like: right and wrong matters; individuals are responsible for their actions; retribution should be swift and sure for those who prey on the innocent.

We must understand that basic moral principles lie at the heart of our criminal justice system; that our system of law acts as the collective moral voice of society.

There's nothing wrong with these values. Nor should we be hesitant or feel guilty about punishing those who violate the elementary rules of civilized existence.

Theft is not a form of political or cultural expression; it is theft, and it is wrong. Murder is not forbidden as a matter of subjective opinion; it is objectively evil, and we must prohibit it. And no one but the thief and murderer benefits when we think and act otherwise.

It has occurred to me that the root causes of our other major domestic problem—the growth of government and the decay of

1

the economy—can be traced to many of the same sources of the crime problem. This is because the same utopian presumptions about human nature that hindered the swift administration of justice have also helped fuel the expansion of government.

Many of the social thinkers of the 1950's and 60's who discussed crime only in the context of disadvantaged childhoods and poverty-stricken neighborhoods were the same people who thought that massive government spending could wipe away our social ills.

The underlying premise in both cases was a belief that there was nothing permanent or absolute about any man's nature—that he was a product of his material environment, and that by changing that environment—with government as the chief vehicle of change through health, housing, and other programs—we could permanently change man and usher in a great new era.

The solution to the crime problem will not be found in the social worker's files, the psychiatrist's notes, or the bureaucrat's budget; it's a problem of the human heart, and it's there we must look for the answer.

We can begin by acknowledging some of those permanent things, those absolute truths I mentioned before.

Two of those truths are that men are basically good but prone to evil; and society has a right to be protected from them.

Only our deep moral values and strong social institutions can ...restrain the darker impulses of human nature.

We have no quarrel with the premise that people should be safe. We do, however, aim to demonstrate that more and swifter punishment of offenders by criminal-justice officials aggravates some of the problem, ignores most of the problem, and generally decreases public safety. If it is the government's business to reduce crime, and we agree that it is, then the government needs to concentrate not so much on law enforcement but on action that strengthens American communities and makes them secure. To do this, Americans have to overcome some basic myths about crime and rethink how government can protect people from thieves and murderers. Much of what we consider common sense about crime is nonsense.

President Reagan says, "There has been a breakdown in the criminal justice system in America. It just plain isn't working." Here is a prime example of sense and nonsense. Yes, it is true that the criminal-justice system is not working, but it is not true that the system has broken down. The system never worked to begin with. As far as can be determined, Americans have suffered as much from crime for nearly two centuries as they do today. There was no golden age of law and order; there was never a time when the police and prisons created more order than disorder in American society. You cannot repair a machine that was never designed to run properly.

The president says that basic moral principles underlie the criminal-justice machine. True, the spirit of law is the moral belief that might does not equal right. The criminal-justice system, however, tells our most heinous criminals that they can get away with theft and murder, that they can violate the spirit of the law with impunity.

Those who kill and steal most in this country know that they are virtually certain not to be arrested, prosecuted, or imprisoned, provided they do it carefully, even professionally. Meanwhile, the members of the group that hurts us least, if for no other reason than that they lack power and means to do harm on the scale that rich folks can manage, are the ones who populate our jails, prisons, and juvenile institutions. American criminal justice is not merely ineffectual; it is also unjust.

This situation endures partly because criminal-justice officials and their sympathizers in the media perpetuate and build myths about crime. The "experts" scare people in the safest neighborhoods into locking themselves behind deadbolt locks, and, by directing attention almost exclusively on the crimes that are easy to see, obscure the fact that Americans face a greater risk of harm in a doctor's office, or a greater risk of ripoff from employees and managers of the stores when they shop, than they do at home or on the street.

If punishment of offenders by criminal-justice officials hurt the guilty and protected the innocent, we would support punishment without hesitation. As it is, punishment generally is inflicted more on the less serious offenders, and it hardly protects victims at all.

People the world over agree that "theft"—taking things from others without their permission —and "murder"— knowingly (rather than accidentally) killing someone— are wrong. But scratch below the surface, and most also agree that some forms of "theft" and "murder" are okay. Indiana law says that it is a felony—punishable by two years in prison and a $10,000 fine—to take a pen home from work for one's own use. But it is not at all unlawful for a corporate manager to close the only factory in town and take away a thousand workers' livelihoods so that shareholders can earn higher dividends and managers higher pay bonuses. By law, it is murder to grant the wish of a terminally ill patient to have a glass of poison to drink, but it is okay for a police officer to shoot a youth who is running down the street with someone else's television set. Lawful or not, these acts are inherently "political," for they constitute exercises of power. And the lines drawn between lawful and unlawful taking and killing are inherently cultural. Just as it is open to legislators to rewrite the law, it is open to citizens to reconsider which kinds of taking and killing they want to define as wrong or right.

We think, for instance, that if the state aims to teach people that stealing is wrong, the state should protect people from having their livelihoods taken. Otherwise, the state may offer its citizens a lesson in absurdity—that taking big things like jobs is right, while taking small things like pens is wrong.

4

Beyond problems of defining the harms themselves lie issues of how to respond to problems. Parents whose child steals from them may demand that the child apologize or work to pay for the loss; they probably will not ask a judge to have this thief adjudicated delinquent and sent to a juvenile institution. Employers commonly ask embezzlers to resign quietly before resorting to calling the police. An alcoholic surgeon who kills a patient on the operating table may be ordered to seek treatment, but will probably not be imprisoned for involuntary manslaughter. When acts are called "crimes," it is implied that the police, courts, and prisons should punish the actors for their misdeeds. But there is a choice. There may be some other more effective ways to handle the problems, and they are used especially when the actors are familiar to the victim or are people of means. Practically every criminal-justice system, including our own, reserves criminalization for chronically unemployed young men, and goes out of its way to leave other people's wrongs to be handled by some other means.

We argue that criminalization is a relatively bad choice for responding to most of the wrongs people do. It is no better choice if an offender is poor or black or young or male. Until options other than imprisonment are explored and used, for rich and poor alike, our government will neither stand for justice nor control crime.

The United States was built on the premise that government intervention does harm to a nation's productive citizens. The Constitution and its amendments offer few guarantees other than that government power will be limited. The Bill of Rights offers no right to work, and no right to be educated or housed.

This does not, however, mean that Americans have rejected big government. On the contrary. If people are unproductive, they are thought of as parasites on private enterprise, parasites that require government intervention and confinement. Just as deterrence of foreign enemies is a sacred service commanding $1,000 per American per year, caging domestic enemies—a smaller but growing sacred service—deserves all-out support. Americans are wary of government that helps provide jobs and training, but embrace government that represses the foreign and the poor.

People like President Reagan do not really oppose big government. Since shortly after the founding of the Republic, state governments and courts have stepped in to absolve owners from personal liability for the wrongs their corporations do, thus encouraging the growth of corporate irresponsibility. President Reagan does not oppose this major government intervention in the economy. Nor does he oppose major forms of tax abatement designed to favor big businesses. He favors growing, sizeable military contracts. He presumably favors greater investment in building prisons and police forces. It is thus a myth that people who oppose redistribution of wealth and power in the American economy favor small government.

We think it clear that the free operation of some kinds of markets slows crime better than the operation of the kind of market the government subsidizes. In fact, the form of government investment in the American economy is crucial to achieving crime control. The government is a part of the American crime problem, and we aim to show how it might instead become a part of the solution.

We agree with the President that Utopian presumptions about human nature have hindered the swift administration of justice. Our country has operated under the Utopian presumption that in a society with a major crime problem criminal-justice officials (who are only human) can administer justice swiftly. Treating too many types of wrongs as police matters makes punishment slow, uncertain, and unjust. And until society accepts this fact, continued frustration over failures to do justice and control crime are inevitable.

We agree, too, that it is mistaken to discuss crime only in the context of disadvantaged childhoods and poverty-stricken neighborhoods. True, the poor get hurt by crime more than the rest of us. But most victimization of poor and rich alike is done by people from advantaged childhoods and rich neighborhoods. Until this fact is recognized, little can be done to ease the plight of the poor.

The program of government reinvestment we outline in the last chapter of this book goes beyond established political ideology of both left and right. Whether the government should invest in curing social ills is a false issue. *How* the government invests in economic and social construction is crucial.

We agree with President Reagan that massive government spending in and of itself is not a cure for social ills. Investment in the MX missile, for instance, massive as that investment may be, will do nothing to prevent crime. And while the poor deserve to eat and stay warm, unemployment compensation or aid to dependent children cannot be expected to "wipe away our social ills" either. Government programs have seldom if ever in American history gone far enough beyond myths about the causes and cures of social ills to treat those ills effectively, regardless of which political party was in control.

We agree wholeheartedly that the solution to the crime problem will not necessarily be found in social workers' files, in psychiatrists' notes, or in the bureaucrat's budget. We agree that people are basically good but socialized to become evil, and that people have a right to have their government protect them from the evil that an unjust society has created. We agree that the United States must proceed from a deep sense of moral values, and that our social institutions need to be strengthened.

Social institutions, however, can hardly be made strong and just as long as Americans proceed on false assumptions about human nature. To be more specific— Americans need to look and move beyond myths about crime and its control. If they can, perhaps a clear way can be found to reduce crime. Our earnest hope is that this book, in which we have confronted and tried to expose these myths, will help do just that.

We owe a great debt to many people for helping us put this book together. Among those we thank are Mary DeShong, Judy Kelley, Vera Marsh, Sheri Perlman and Andrew Vorder Bruegge for typing; Gil Geis, Stash Baronett, Larry Salinger, Henry Pontell, Karen and Jennifer McClung, Bob Bryant, Jill Bystydzienski, and Katy Pepinsky for general support and encouragement; and Calvin Kytle and the editors of Seven Locks Press for helping us move from rough manuscript to the printed page.

Harold E. Pepinsky
Paul Jesilow
Bloomington, Indiana
June 1984

Introduction

There is much crime in America, more than ever is reported, far more than ever is solved, far too much for the health of the Nation. Every American knows that. Every American is, in a sense, a victim of crime. Violence and theft have not only injured, often irreparably, hundreds of thousands of citizens, but have directly affected everyone. Some people have been impelled to uproot themselves and find new homes. Some have been made afraid to use public streets and parks. Some have come to doubt the worth of a society in which so many people behave so badly. Some have become distrustful of the Government's ability, or even desire, to protect them. Some have lapsed into the attitude that criminal behavior is normal human behavior and consequently have become indifferent to it, or have adopted it as a good way to get ahead in life. Some have become suspicious of those they conceive to be responsible for crime: adolescents or Negroes or drug addicts or college students or demonstrators; policemen who fail to solve crimes; judges who pass lenient sentences or write decisions restricting the activities of the police; parole boards that release prisoners who resume their criminal activities.

The most understandable mood into which many

9

Americans have been plunged by crime is one of frustration and bewilderment. For "crime" is not a single simple phenomenon that can be examined, analyzed and described in one piece. It occurs in every part of the country and in every stratum of society. Its practitioners and its victims are people of all ages, incomes and backgrounds. Its trends are difficult to ascertain. Its causes are legion. Its cures are speculative and controversial. An examination of any single kind of crime, let alone of "crime in America," raises a myriad of issues of the utmost complexity.

President's Commission on Law Enforcement and Administration of Justice, 1967

THE SOONER we recognize that criminal justice is a state-protection racket, the better. State power confronts citizens' power. The result is practically inevitable: punishment most hurts the citizens who have the least power to hurt others or to resist arrest, conviction, or imprisonment—the children of the chronically unemployed underclass. The poor and dispossessed bear the brunt of the public fervor to punish; other people equally or more deserving of punishment remain untouched.

This compulsion to scapegoat the poor has followed a pattern for at least four centuries in Europe and North America. It intensifies during periods of high unemployment, when organized tradespeople decry unfair competition of cheap convict labor (or foreign labor), and when political leaders announce that those who fall by the economic wayside will have to pull themselves together, aided perhaps by private charity. High unemployment parallels business failure; so owners, managers, and workers alike fear for their careers. The need to accommodate one's superiors is self-evident; one dares not blame

10

them for one's troubles. In a society with a sizeable middle class, common agreement on whom to blame for anxious times settles on the underclass; crime is seen as a depravity that breeds and is bred by poverty.

Each year in the U.S., the number of arrests of non-white men in their twenties is exactly the same as the number of non-white men in their twenties. About one in seventeen of the men in this demographic group is spending today in jail or prison. Add in those on probation or parole, and one in five non-white men in their twenties is in some form of criminal-justice custody.

The proportion of the American population incarcerated increased by 140 percent between 1973 and 1983. While less than one in 3,000 Americans was locked up in 1850, one in 270 is incarcerated in some form of punitive institution today. The United States has become one of the world's most punitive societies, and the trend is getting worse.

The U.S. pays a lot to punish. Police and corrections cost about $100 per American per year; private security measures another $100. People believe crime is at a record high, and many are paralyzed by fear. We put extra locks all over our homes and dare not venture onto the streets at night. The fear of crime has become a major source of agoraphobia—fear of participating in civic life. If security is what we pay criminal-justice officials to give us, criminal justice is one of the services for which we pay more to accomplish less.

During nineteenth-century depressions the poor were called "the dangerous class." In today's police jargon they are the "criminal element" or "the perpetrators." The problem is that our livelihood and position remain at risk and our anxiety continues to mount no matter how much the underclass is punished. Committed to the belief that the underclass is the chief threat, people accept media,

11

official, and scholarly assertions that the crime problem is grotesque and worsening. When mass murder occurs halfway across the American continent, each is prone to fear that he or she will be the next victim. And so more is paid for "protection," and further prison overcrowding is all that the extra money accomplishes.

The more aggressively police go after poor young men, the more law enforcement highlights the relative impunity with which persons of means can prey upon others. With so many resources committed to patrolling the streets, activities in the suites may go practically unnoticed. (As criminologist Stanley Pennington points out, hidden victimization is the hallmark of consumer fraud.) Wealthier people can get away with a multitude of crimes before their activities are even questioned. Steady employment conveys an aura of respectability, serving to reinforce a self-image that rarely includes one's own acts of crime. The business executive in a Brooks Brothers suit who denies another a pay raise to provide himself with a chauffer-driven limousine neither perceives himself nor is perceived as a thief, in part because society has cast him in a role far removed from that of the stereotyped underclass fiend and because the nature of his crime makes it difficult to pinpoint a victim.

Forty years of "self-report" surveys show that by late adolescence, most of us have become chronic offenders; almost all of us break the law. Perhaps it does no great harm to make personal use of some supplies one gets at work. Perhaps one's neighbors can afford to lose a little sleep during a loud party. Perhaps one can drive or walk home unscathed after having had a few too many drinks. As familiar as such behavior is to many in everyday life, it is also the routine stuff of criminal court dockets. People live with and commit the great bulk of what could be treated as crime without making a big deal of it, with no thought of involving the police or the courts, with no thought of jailing others or being jailed.

Most can identify really terrible people they have worked or lived around, and it is easy to identify really heinous street criminals. But what distinguishes the normal defendant or prisoner is not that his behavior is so much more outrageous than the behavior of "respectable" citizens, but that his political and economic position is so low.

Some people suggest that punishment of criminals ought to be extended to include persons of means. After all, they argue, white-collar offenders are more deterrable by punishment than the poor whose very poverty is a punishment that has already failed to deter wrongful behavior. Extension of punishment, however, has two inescapable problems. First, since any criminal-justice system is inherently political, it is virtually inconceivable that enforcement could be organized so as to be balanced between have-nothings and powerful citizens. Second, crime is so pervasive that if full enforcement were approached, practically all would be in and out of jail; there would be precious few law-abiding citizens to police the rest. The U.S. has to turn elsewhere for progress in crime control. Among wealthier citizens, grievances are not treated as crime, and matters resolve easily. If underclass youth were extended the same privilege, the protection money paid to criminal justice could be better spent elsewhere.

Exposing Myths About Crime

Criminal-justice policy and practice is built on a centuries-old body of assumptions that a number of leading criminologists continue to propagate. Much of it is nonsense, founded on seldom-questioned myths about how criminal justice functions and what it can achieve. If American crime control is to be turned from failure, the wrongness and emptiness of its major myths need to be exposed and understood. If and when Americans see that their police, their courts and their prisons do little good and much injustice, they may prove willing to reinvest their money in more promising enterprises.

Ten major myths about crime and justice are discussed in this book:

Myth 1: Crime is increasing. One obvious justification for more criminal justice is that Americans are suffering more crime and need more official relief. But are Americans in more danger from crime today than they have been in the past? The evidence is not clear that they are, or that they suffer from crime nearly as much as commonly supposed. Still police and the media have scared us into believing that our streets have become too dangerous to walk and have frightened us into paying more and more money for law enforcement.

Myth 2: Most crime is committed by the poor. The poor get into trouble with the law far more than the rich. Some people argue that the poor deserve the most punishment because they commit the most crime. In fact, it appears that the rich unlawfully hurt their fellow citizens far more than the poor do. Punishment of offenders constitutes a morally unjustifiable form of economic discrimination.

Myth 3: Some groups are more law-abiding than others. Okay, the rich get away with more crime than the poor, but it is argued that apart from a few rotten apples in professions with high emphasis on ethics, some groups are more honest and law abiding than others. This chapter describes the criminality encouraged by the structure of American medical care. As matters stand, no group is immune from substantial criminality.

14

Myth 4: White-collar crime is nonviolent. It is generally held that even if the rich commit more crime, it is the poor who commit the most serious, the violent offenses. But it turns out that the white-collar and organizational crimes kill far more people than do street criminals. Jeffrey Reiman, in *The Rich Get Richer and the Poor Get Prison*, provides strong evidence that well over 100,000 criminal homicides are committed annually by respected professionals.

Myth 5: Regulatory agencies prevent white-collar crime. It is commonly argued that considerations of social justice ought to give way to being practical about protecting citizens from crime. After all, administrative regulation protects society from the transgressions of the rich, and criminal justice is necessary to hold down street crime. In reality, even when victims and regulatory agencies are aware of criminality (which most often they are not), regulators' effectiveness is impaired by numerous factors. Thus, claims that white-collar wrongdoing is checked by sanctions are wrong.

Myth 6: Rich and poor are equal before the law. In truth, the wealthy have the capacity to protect themselves against prosecution, and the invisibility of their crimes prevents detection. Equity would require that almost all police resources be used to look for crime in the business suites rather than crime in the streets. Furthermore, if arrested, the poor are less likely to get out of jail before trial, more likely to be convicted, and more likely to be imprisoned if convicted. Criminal justice is inherently discriminatory. The less criminal justice acts, the more social justice is promoted.

Myth 7: Drug addiction causes crime. Drug addiction is mythologized as one of the major causes of violence and street crime. Actually, addiction to drugs doesn't cause society or the addict nearly as much harm as is supposed.

Myth 8: Community corrections is a viable alternative. It has been thought that the best way to help an offender integrate into law-abiding communities is community-treatment programs. But, community-corrections programs have turned out to be feeding grounds for standard criminal justice, rather than substitutes. Once again, legal repression of crime is part of the crime problem, not a solution.

Myth 9: The punishment can fit the crime. Is there a moral obligation to hurt those who hurt others whether or not the punishment helps to stop crime? Perhaps, but nobody can dole out punishments in defense of morality because the punishment cannot be made to fit the crime. When crime becomes prevalent, popular consensus on how much harm a crime entails is impossible to achieve. Moreover, crime overloads the criminal-justice system so that swiftness, sureness, and severity of punishment cannot be controlled.

Myth 10: Law makes people behave. Despite the gross failure to control crime through law enforcement, Americans are generally honest and peaceful. Does the law keep them that way? What social conditions make people more or less civil toward one another? We know that people are restrained by private social ties more than by legal commands. Greater resort to criminal justice is a sign that social ties, at home and at work, are unreliable. To reduce crime, we need to turn away from prisons and all other correctional facilities that help break societal ties, and toward community organizations that strengthen ties.

What Makes Law Enforcement Grow?

The worse a law enforcement agency does, the more funds it commands. If law enforcement actually worked—

actually lessened crime—fewer of its officials would be needed. Police, sheriffs and their deputies, prosecutors, judges, probation and parole officers, court clerks and stenographers, public defenders, counselors, prison officials, and criminologists all depend on fear of crime for their livelihoods.

Economic pressures for all public services to expand is particularly strong when jobs are tight and increased employment by a public agency like law enforcement effectively reduces competition in the private job market. Less than half a century after the United States was founded, the supply of labor was already beginning to expand faster than the number of jobs. Now that we have learned to replace workers with robots, the employment of human beings is becoming more and more unnecessary. We have discovered two ways to handle the problem. One is to create service jobs, the other is to confine the number of would-be competitors for the few positions available.

This book focuses on crime and criminal justice, but it is important to recognize that crime-fighting is not the only confinement industry. Schooling is the biggest. American schooling was first made compulsory in the mid-1800s, and during the 1900s the number of years of schooling that people needed to qualify for jobs escalated, so that more people were kept out of the job market longer. Before he could practice law today, Abraham Lincoln would have to finish high school, complete four years of college, and go to law school for three years just to qualify to take the bar examination. Once it took a high-school diploma to qualify for a good job, then a college degree. Now even a doctorate—let alone the increasingly obsolete master's degree—may not suffice.

As a way of restricting the job market, however, confinement by criminal justice has an advantage over that provided by schooling. More even than ex-mental patients, ex-offenders are effectively barred from good jobs for life. Some succeed, to be sure, but against long odds. Convicted felons may not be allowed to vote, let alone be licensed for any number of occupations. Most states bar a former burglar from cutting hair. Even without licensing restrictions, the stigma of a criminal record is enough to keep ex-offenders from being hired, and to justify social rejection.

These days, it is a bit out of fashion to act against injustice on principle; practicality is the order of the day. No matter. Today's costly war on crime is not only a blatant act of class discrimination but, since it fails to address the most basic, pervasive, and unlawful threats to our personal and economic security, it cannot and will not alleviate crime or the fear of crime. This is not only the fault of criminal-justice officials; it is the peoples' fault for expecting from law enforcement what it cannot deliver.

Americans invest one dollar of every seventy on public and private security while law enforcement becomes more top-heavy, centralized, and technologized. Citizens receive minimal personal benefit from leaving their security in professional hands. Those hurt by crime lose power to recoup their losses as officials gain power to punish offenders. American anthropologist Phil Parnell and Norwegian sociologist Nils Christie point out that the power at issue is the power to manage disputes—either by separating the parties (as by taking them off to jail), or negotiating a way for them to be co-contributors to some social enterprise from which each receives palpable benefits. Police and citizens are capable of separating disputants. But parties to the dispute have to take it on themselves to become partners in a common enterprise and to solve the problems between them before either will be able to receive any real compensation.

Beyond Myth

Power and status nowadays rest heavily on the ability to control access to machines—the more complex the machine the better. A sign of presidential power is control over the computer system of the National Security Agency. Philosophers of science have long since isolated three basic requisites of mastering knowledge: that the patterns of data (theories) be consistant (or reliable), simple (or parsimonious) and fruitful (produce useful results). As long as we remain preoccupied with expanding the inventory of complexity we control, we ignore the virtue of simplicity. A gain in simplicity means that a broader range of people can master use of the knowledge—can use the technology. The harder the line between those who can and cannot use it, the more its function will be lost to non-users.

It is no coincidence that levels of unemployment correspond to levels of crime. Jobs, like the successful negotiation of disputes, depend on the availability of common enterprise; and imprisonment largely amounts to punishment for being jobless. To deal with both crime and unemployment, the parsimonious solution lies in the direction of government investment in creating worker-owned enterprises throughout society and employing technology that ordinary citizens can control themselves—in author E. F. Schumacher's terms, *appropriate* technology. Technological development, therefore, ought to be applied to the simplest problems that can be managed by the widest number of participants, and this should be the primary objective of a government that aims both to contain crime and to put people to work. The section "Beyond Myth" describes how the U. S. government might turn in this direction.

Each year, Americans opt to extend investment in

criminal justice and private security. They might begin investing some of this money and effort in measures of social control that are positive, empowering, and liberating. This book ends by proposing some specific activities for such investment.

Police cannot take care of crime. Crime can be taken care of only if we move beyond myth.

MYTH ONE

"Crime is increasing."

There has always been too much crime. Virtually every generation since the founding of the Nation and before has felt itself threatened by the spectre of rising crime and violence.

A hundred years ago contemporary accounts of San Francisco told of extensive areas where "no decent man was in safety to walk the street after dark; while at all hours, both night and day, his property was jeopardized by incendiarism and burglary." Teenage gangs gave rise to the word "hoodlum"; while in one central New York City area, near Broadway, the police entered "only in pairs, and never unarmed." A noted chronicler of the period declared that "municipal law is a failure...we must soon fall back on the law of self preservation." Alarming increases in robbery and violent crimes were reported throughout the country prior to the Revolution. And, in 1910, one author declared that "crime, especially its more violent forms and among the young, is increasing steadily and is threatening to bankrupt the Nation..."

*President's Commission
on Law Enforcement and
Administration of Justice, 1967*

ACCOUNTS OF LIFE in the urban centers of the late 1800s and early 1900s are hair raising. Crime was a real threat, but then as now the picture of the crime problem painted by official crime statistics was seriously distorted. Persons today might know that their home and those of others around them have been broken into more often in the past few months or year. But they cannot know whether their experience is isolated, is compensated for by drops in crime in other areas, or is typical of trends in American communities. So, the distorted image created by criminal-justice officials with sleight-of-hand and statistics can easily persuade the homeowner that their home is imperiled by an advancing horde of hoodlums. In reality, a careful study of crime statistics yields no reason to believe that overall street crime has been rising; people today are in no greater danger of being robbed or physically hurt than 150 years ago.

Americans, however, have been all too willing to accept the myth that crime is increasing. Virtually all believe that an already excessive crime problem has grown two or three times larger during the last twenty years and that the threat to our lives and property has become a crisis. Thus, communities feel the need to pay ever-increasing amounts to stem the flood of criminality. Criminal-justice officials and the news media help spread this belief: the former to get more money for their various departments, the latter to have something to fill its front pages and news broadcasts.

Counting Crime

It was Enlightenment thinking of the eighteenth century that caused people to think that crime might be subject to rational management. Until then, it had been thought important to keep only records of criminal trials and these only for purposes of appeal. In the late 1700s, however, Jeremy Bentham proposed that the moral health of a society could be gauged by how much crime occurred. If crime were rising, he argued, government could turn the tide by raising the cost of crime.

So in the 1820s England, France and some American states (beginning in New York in 1829) began to calculate the numbers and types of crimes for which defendants were convicted. When conviction rates rose, it was assumed that depravity was overtaking society.

There are two major problems with the assumption that convictions indicate the amount of crime in a jurisdiction: the problems of overstatement and understatement. Criminologists and politicians have been consumed with problems of understatement. By the late 1800s commentators pointed out that many crimes never resulted in prosecution, let alone conviction, and a large "dark figure" of unreported or "hidden" crime haunted their existence.

The problem of exaggeration has received only recent and sporadic attention. It occurs in two ways. First, officials can suddenly spring into action and bring more defendants to trial; what is reported as an increase in crime can be a simple reflection of a burst of government energy. Second, innocent people can and do get convicted of crime. At Ohio State University, Arye Ratner has collected newspaper accounts of several hundred cases over the last fifty years in which convicted people were later found innocent. He cites one estimate that 14,000 people are wrongfully convicted in U.S. courts every year. Given our reluctance to concede that courts can convict innocent people, this might well be an understatement.

Most of the cases Ratner reviewed involved conviction of the wrong people, but almost anybody who has ever been with police or in a court room is also aware of cases in which citizens are charged and prosecuted where no crimes at all have occurred. For instance, people have been known to plead guilty to disturbing the peace when they have done no more than lawfully challenge a police officer's request to see identification. Defendants who cannot afford bail are likely to plead guilty, not as an admission of guilt, but simply to get out of jail without having to wait for trial, particularly for the minor charges that form the bulk of court business. We really have no idea how many people are convicted of these phantom offenses, but the number could be substantial.

The Game of Crime Statistics

There were no uniformed police forces when government began compiling conviction statistics. When police came into being in the middle of the nineteenth century, they immediately started keeping records of not only how many people were convicted, but also how many they arrested. It didn't take long for these statistics to be used for police ends. As early as 1858, a New York police chief used increased arrest records for political purposes. He told the City Council that the city was caught in a crime wave that could be controlled only by the expansion of manpower.

There are few enterprises in which people can hope to be supported more for accomplishing less. Police are hired in the hope they will prevent and contain crime, and yet it is by demonstrating their failure to do so—by showing that the crime problem is larger than ever—that they can best argue for expansion. There is a standing joke among criminologists that if they found a way to eliminate crime, they would be out of a job. This was the insight that the

New York City Chief of Police achieved in 1858. Arrest figures have been used in the same way ever since.

In the 1960s, police departments across the country established drug units, causing drug arrests to mount. The police used arrest data to show that drug abuse was becoming a major American problem, and went so far as to attribute the rise in other forms of crime to mounting drug abuse. Now in the face of budget cuts, federal drug enforcers have succeeded in convincing President and Mrs. Reagan that the drug problem has mushroomed, requiring new infusions of federal support. Of course, how much the amount of illicit drug traffic has increased is determined by how much officials find; and, how much they find depends on how hard they look. Recent surveys indicate that the use of some drugs, like marijuana, may have decreased over the past decade. But, officials have an investment in demonstrating that the problem they are hired to control is less manageable, and their play on citizen fears carries enormous political weight.

Arrest data like conviction statistics eventually were dismissed as inadequate. In 1911, Louis Newton Robinson published a widely cited critique of crime measurement, arguing in part that arrest figures themselves vastly understated the crime problem. After all, he pointed out, many crimes occurred in which no suspect was identified. It would be far better, although still imperfect, to rely on police counts of all reported offenses regardless of whether arrests followed. In 1927, the International Association of Chiefs of Police recommended that nationwide reports of "offenses known to the police" be compiled, and three years later the Federal Bureau of Investigation began soliciting these figures from law enforcement agencies. To this day, the FBI annually publishes the *Uniform Crime Reports*, which features

25

compilation of known offenses among what are called "Index" or "Part I" offenses. The list of Index Offenses changes periodically. In 1978, arson was added to the existing list of murder/non-negligent manslaughter; aggravated assault; robbery (including attempts); rape (including attempts); burglary (including attempts); auto theft and all other thefts.

The FBI has been particularly ingenious at using these reports. In the 1930s it reported increases in the number of crimes committed without acknowledging that the number of enforcement agencies responding to FBI surveys had increased substantially. Although the FBI later corrected this error, it found other ways to emphasize the growth of crime. Reported crime rates declined from 1971 to 1972. The FBI's *Uniform Crime Reports* for 1972, however, didn't say that. It went back to 1969 to report that crime increased from 1969 to 1972. When crime rates began to rise again, the FBI used 1972 as a base year to make increases seem larger. Similar machinations were used to draw attention from the decreases reported for 1976 and 1977. In fact, in its presentation of 1976 figures, the FBI reported percentage trends only for 1972 to 1975, implying that the 1976 decrease was less than significant.

During World War II and then Korea, when American attention was turned toward foreign fronts and many of the law enforcement officials and potential criminals were overseas, police-reported rates declined or remained steady. Police were concentrating on what noted criminologist Albert Reiss has called "proactive enforcement," the detecting of offenses primarily in the areas of traffic enforcement, vice-squad activity, and in street gang activity; the best and brightest criminologists of the period were paid to study why gang members went bad.

After Korea, urban police departments around the country dramatically changed enforcement priorities. The police suddenly became "reactive." People were urged to call the police to report any suspicious activity, and the police were mobilized to respond. In Indianapolis in 1956, a new chief of police equipped motorcycles with radios so that select officers could respond to traffic accidents, and changed two-men patrol cars to one-man cars newly equipped with three-way radios. Shortly afterward, new communications systems were introduced to speed response to citizens' calls for assistance. The media promoted the police appeals for cooperation, and in return the police promised that they could wipe out the scourge of crime. Data from American and British police departments show that in the 1950s and during similar police campaigns, calls for police service have skyrocketed.

Over the years police have succeeded in convincing the American public of the need for bigger and better enforcement, but a generation of bigger crime figures proved a mixed blessing. As crime rose, the police drew fire for failing to deliver on their promise to eliminate the problem through vigorous enforcement. The police could not say that the increases were due to changes in reporting practices without jeopardizing their claimed need for more resources. From time to time, the police experimented with cutting crime reports back. Again, the experience in Indianapolis illustrates. After charges of corruption had demoralized the force, a new, young, reform-minded police chief entered office in 1968 in a burst of enthusiasm. Once again, citizens were enlisted in the war on crime, and reported crime shot up, leading to press reports that the police were losing the war. In 1969 the police reorganized their records office and reported a drop in crime. In high spirits, the police again enlisted citizens to help continue the progress toward stamping out crime, causing crime reports to jump back up in 1970. Under fire for failing to make progress in the war on crime despite a new infusion of federal funds, the police reported less crime in, 1971, then more in 1972. By 1976, Indianapolis newspapers had become wary and weary of police claims. When another new chief who was promoting the current federally supported crime prevention programs reported less crime for 1976, he was taken to task.

A major device used to give the impression that crime was being reduced was to increase "unfounding" rates. Within FBI guidelines, law enforcement agencies are entitled to take crime reports off their books if further police investigation reveals that the offense has not occurred; this is called "unfounding." The Indianapolis Police Department's unfounding rate had been 5.4 percent in 1971, had grown to 12.9 percent in 1975, and had become 19.8 percent in 1976. The chief attributed the increase to a statistician, hired in October 1975, who was "doing a more thorough job."

One example of "thoroughness" concerned burglary. The FBI asks for burglaries to be classified by whether they have occurred during the day or at night. In many circumstances, complainants or the police are unable to determine when the burglaries happened. Prior to October 1975, these reports were divided between day- and nighttime classifications, but afterward the statistician unfounded them all on the grounds that there was no category for them on FBI forms.

The press began to report other artifice as well. For instance, in an area in which the police were publicizing a holiday patrol, a supervisor instructed a patrol officer to reclassify a break-in with $4,000 loss from burglary (an Index Offense) to trespass (a non-compiled misdemeanor). Similar instructions to officers around the country have been reported during crime prevention campaigns.

Even murder/non-negligent manslaughter is subject to manipulation. Beginning in the mid-1960s, the medical examiner of Hamilton County, Ohio, raised homicide figures substantially by doing routine autopsies in new categories of cases (notably infants who had been brought to hospital emergency rooms, and of corpses found in cars and in bathtubs). For their part, in 1974 the Indiana police reported that they had "cleared" (as by arresting suspects) 105.5 homicides for every 100 reported. Asked to explain such figures, an officer in the research and planning division explained that offenses might sometimes be unfounded when the prosecutor declined to proceed (in violation of FBI guidelines). Arrests, however, remained on the books or were carried over to a new year. Given that the FBI defines murder/non-negligent manslaughter to include killing in self-defense or with other justification (unless the justified killer is a police officer), the police have considerable discretion to decide whether a homicide calls for a report of an Index Offense.

In a climate of concern that the crime problem was understated, in 1965 the President's Commission on Law Enforcement and Administration of Justice commissioned three sets of community surveys, in which samples of residents and businesses were asked whether they had been victimized by crime. Published in 1967, the surveys indicated that Index crime was more than twice as high as reported by police. Furthermore, a couple of reverse record checks showed that many victims who had previously responded to surveys had failed to report a substantial number of offenses.

It has been argued that since police figures remain well below victimization rates, police are only catching up to where they should be in responding to crime. This overlooks the issue of whether more police protection is needed now than was needed a decade or a hundred years ago. The question is not how much crime there is but whether the police affect the amount of crime. Why pay millions of dollars for unneeded services?

Each year since 1973 the Bureau of the Census, in cooperation with the Department of Justice, has conducted victim surveys of national samples of American residents, covering all Index Offenses except murder/non-negligent manslaughter and arson. The kicker is that, except for some rise in theft and assault rates, the victim surveys showed a decline in all offenses whereas the police were reporting dramatic increases in these same offenses. A British Home Office study of burglary and theft finds the same for England and Wales, adding that victim survey respondents also were reporting no more offenses to police at the end of the 1970s than at the beginning (as opposed to increases in police *recording* of offenses).

All in all, when one looks at historians' descriptions of violence and predation in nineteenth-century American communities, one wonders whether today's communities are not relatively trouble-free. At the very least, there is no demonstration that Americans are in more danger from unlawful behavior than they were then. What is clear is that criminal justice has grown tremendously, and that statistical artifice has been used as a major tool for convincing Americans that the threat of crime has escalated. It is questionable whether Americans need more police protection now than ever; it is unquestionable that criminologists and officials have conspired to make it appear that way.

Proactive discovery of offenses remains something of a liability to police. Historian Eric Monkkonen reports that public-order arrests, as for morals offenses and disorderly conduct, fell off from 1860 to 1920, and although such arrests still predominate in American police work, they are also falling today. When the police enforce the law on their own initiative, they alone are held responsible for the resulting unpleasantness. When the Indianapolis police launched vice and traffic crackdowns in the early years of the 1950s, 1960s, and 1970s, public antagonism and suspicion of police activity created scandal. The press burst forth with allegations of police corruption resulting in indictments for bribery and demoralization in police ranks.

On the other hand, unless citizens cooperate with the police by providing complaints, the police will remain limited in their ability to find crime. Furthermore, when increased enforcement results from response to citizen complaints, the public shares the responsibility. Therefore, police welcome complaints from the community, which serve to remove some of the risk of public recrimination. But, it is not at all obvious that citizens should call in complaints in response to police entreaties. Were communities tightly knit and secure, contact with police would be avoided except in the most destructive or violent of cases. Among the world's peoples, however, Americans are quite loosely knit and insecure, inclined to trust police and outside professionals.

In the middle of the nineteenth century, a young Frenchman named Alexis de Tocqueville wrote a comprehensive analysis of the American way of life called *Democracy in America*, which remains widely recognized as one of the more insightful descriptions of American political culture. In it he wrote about the kind of despotism the archetypal democratic nation had to fear. He found Americans incredibly preoccupied with individual material gain. They saw demands for group cooperation and involvement as impediments to personal advancement—if not a threat, then at least a nuisance. When it came to

31

political affairs, Americans were predisposed to remain aloof from debate over issues. They could be expected to give mandates to politicians who pretended expertise to manage their social affairs. American government could become despotic by popular default.

People seem most inclined to trust their business to outside experts in societies where geographical and social mobility is high, that is, where people change social ties frequently in families (as through divorce and through children moving away from parents), in residence (by moving), and at work (by changing jobs or being unemployed). The United States ranks highest in the world in these types of mobility. Some kinds, like changes of residence, have been high throughout the history of the Republic; others, like divorce rates, have increased fourfold since the beginning of this century.

This type of mobility is linked to a course of economic development in which a premium is placed on increasing efficiency by replacing human labor with sophisticated machines. Under these conditions, training and production become centralized, standardized, and subject to rapid change and dislocation. To get ahead, even to keep up, people have to move around to hold jobs.

As people move, those they live and work with become more like undependable strangers. Expedience in personal relations, doing unto others before they do unto you, becomes conventional wisdom. Greater anonymity makes it increasingly possible to get away with violence and predation. When one suffers loss or pain, family members, neighbors and co-workers are less likely to have the time or the understanding to lend a sympathetic ear. Those who are paid to give aid and comfort, from the therapist to the welfare worker to the police officer, become more dependable than one's acquaintances. When disputes break out, one is less likely to feel able to confront the other party directly; trusted family members, neighbors or co-workers are unavailable or untrusted as mediators; mechanisms for handling disputes privately are absent. If, for example, someone in the next apartment is playing loud music, one will be less likely to ask the neighbor to turn it down before calling the police.

These circumstances predispose citizens and criminal-justice officials alike to embrace all evidence that the crime problem is understated, and to be skeptical of evidence that it is exaggerated. Americans have been remarkably willing to buy into the law enforcement protection racket.

What Is Crime?

It should be clear by now that crime is not purely and simply harmful behavior. To begin with, the law is rather arbitrary about what kinds of harm are regarded as crime. It can be considered criminal to refuse to kill, as conscientious objectors have discovered during wartime. It can be legally tolerable to kill, in self-defense or in defense of property. On the other hand, it may be regarded as unlawful to help a terminally ill person in great pain to commit suicide. Common sense and compassion are often missing in the law's definition of what is permissible.

The application of the law is highly restrictive. Philosopher of criminal justice David Reiman indicates that more than four times as many people may be killed unlawfully by unnecessary surgery and criminal disregard of worker safety and health than are murdered. While the FBI reported that property loss from street crime was $4 billion per year, minimum estimate of customer loss from white-collar crime was $40 billion. To equalize the chances of the crimes of rich and poor being detected and pursued, it would be wise to allocate 99 police officers to investigate corporate suites for every officer patrolling the streets. In self-report studies, practically every person responding admits to having committed offenses periodically, and so full enforcement would probably require that almost every American go to jail or prison from time to time.

Under these circumstances, it is impossible to conclude that the harm and loss we suffer at the hands of others bears any relation to crime trends. Even where disputes are recognized, people often resolve them privately (e.g., talking to the parents of a child who has thrown a rock through one's window) rather than treating them as crimes. Crime statistics are not reliable indicators of harmful behavior, but can only be presumed to indicate peoples' willingness to have incidents managed by criminal-justice officials. *Crime statistics, then, tell us how citizens and officials are responding to crime, but not how big the crime problem itself is.*

"Most crime is committed by the poor."

Among a million people, such as compose the population of this city and its suburbs, there will always be a great number of misfortunes; fathers die, and leave their children unprovided for; parents drink, and abuse their little ones, and they float away on the currents of the street; stepmothers or stepfathers drive out, by neglect and ill treatment, their sons from home. Thousands are the children of poor foreigners, who have permitted their children to grow up without school, education, or religion. All the neglect and bad education and evil example of a poor class tend to form others, who, as they mature, swell the ranks of ruffians and criminals. So, at length, a great multitude of ignorant, untrained, passionate, irreligious boys and young men are formed, who become the "dangerous class" of our city.

Charles Loring Brace, 1872

IN THE BURGEONING CITIES of industrializing America of the nineteenth century, the poor were known as "the dangerous class." As they bore children, so presumably, they bred criminality. Even Karl Marx denounced them in 1848 in the *Communist Manifesto* as "social scum, that

35

passively rotting mass thrown off by the lower layers of society.''

The explanations for criminality's association with the poor were many and varied, and sound remarkably familiar today. Some believed that criminality was an inherited trait, or that criminality stemmed from being uneducated in middle-class virtues. Others felt that the physical conditions of poverty, like malnutrition and disease, led to moral depravity. Poverty was blamed for broken homes, which in turn caused children to grow up wrong. Many believed that the poor were forced to steal to eat, or that they were moved to take shortcuts to the good life of the middle class. Some theorized that criminality spread like an infectious disease—that by growing up among criminals, youths copied the criminal's lifestyle, or that by growing up detached from stable rural environments they developed no respect for social order. The theory that unemployed youths become undisciplined through idleness was one basis for making schooling compulsory in mid-century and sending those who were truant or in trouble to special training schools. It was believed that the foreignness of poor immigrants caused a lack of understanding of Anglo-Saxon virtues. Some believed that poor criminals were rebels against economic exploitation, and some reformers believed that, however poor youth got into trouble with the law initially, putting them in prison only taught them to be confirmed offenders.

Poverty as Failure

After fighting a principled war for national independence, Americans had a high stake in believing that their government was essentially fair. It was supposed that, by requiring little of citizens other than that they refrain from infringing one another's rights to life, liberty, and property, the Constitution assured that individuals of equal energy and talent would enjoy the opportunity to rise to the same height in the social order. Pure merit would be rewarded in the Republic; aristocracy was a thing of the past.

The trouble was that in the land of opportunity, some groups persistently failed to move up the economic ladder. Over the long run, one group of poor might be displaced by others—Germans by Irish; Irish by Asians; Southern and Eastern Europeans by blacks, Hispanics, and Native Americans. But, in the short run, the children, especially of the urban poor, largely remained destitute, and in turn bore destitute offspring. This phenomenon has been well documented in recent years, in a pair of studies by sociologists Peter Blau and Otis Dudley Duncan (1962), and Robert Hauser and David Featherman (1973). While sons in these two surveys generally tended to move to higher class occupations than their fathers, the greatest percentage of black sons of fathers in all categories—including those in "upper white-collar" jobs—moved to lower-class manual occupations. Among the chronically unemployed, underclass non-whites persist in having double the unemployment rate of whites; about half of non-white youths remain jobless. Class divisions are clearest and firmest when the job market stagnates, as it first did within a half century after the founding of the nation. How could it be that this central feature of aristocratic order remained true of the revolutionary order? Americans who prospered could not believe that the political foundations of their society were fundamentally flawed. It followed, then, that the poor must suffer from some form of personal defect that prevented them from prospering in a society created so all citizens could thrive.

Western society has alternated between two reactions to the supposed infirmities of the poor. One reaction has been to punish the poor for their sins, the other to treat them for their sickness. As a rule, not only in the United States but in Europe for at least several centuries, punishment prevails in periods of high employment, and charity or treatment prevails when the supply of jobs exceeds the demand. Here again in the mid-1980s, it is time to be punitive. The poor are regarded as being too lazy to go out and find jobs listed in the want ads, and too undisciplined to respect the law.

The alternative does the poor no great favor. In a society where so many believe that those who succeed do so by the merit of their own efforts, special treatment further stigmatizes those already regarded as socially disabled. What a person achieves with help from others is suspect, and the recipient of treatment has to work all the harder to overcome the presumption that help has given him or her an unfair advantage over others. Women and minorities who have been hired under affirmative action programs are commonly regarded as incompetent and less qualified for their jobs; former mental patients are commonly regarded as liabilities once removed from the crutch of treatment; and former inmates are regarded as untrustworthy for having gotten along only when people were watching and helping them. Unlike some other societies, where welfare benefits like health care, unemployment compensation, and aid to children are fundamental rights of all citizens, the American society considers welfare degrading; recipients are deemed less than adequate people for accepting it. As the cycle has swung from punishment (or discipline) to treatment to punishment over the past century-and-a-half, Americans have been repeatedly distressed to find that, despite their best efforts, the poor have remained poor, sick, and crippled.

38

If the poor have not responded by becoming rich and successful, it is believed that they must be too degenerate to benefit from aid or instruction. The failure of government to deal successfully with poverty simply confirms the premise that the poor are subhuman.

American View of Poverty

People do not start with equal social endowment. A country might approach equal social opportunity if all children were conceived in laboratories and raised by professionals in common institutions, in a classless *Brave New World*. It might be possible to divorce success from the socio-economic status of biological parents if all newborns were randomly reallocated among families. As matters stand, children of the poor are unlikely to be given generous allowances to invest for their future, or to grow up experiencing the manners and skills equated with wealth and leadership ability. Given the same genetic endowment, it is obvious that a poor child would have to expend much greater effort than a rich twin to achieve success and affluence. It is a wondrous self-deception which allows Americans to believe that merit will achieve its just reward.

A corollary absurdity is the belief that people's merit can and should be measured on a single scale, as by I.Q. or wealth. A medical doctor who is a wonderful diagnostician may not be resourceful enough to feed a family on a small welfare check without cash reserves or a credit rating. One great mistake many make is to assume that poor school performance implies intellectual inferiority. It can take a lot of talent and skill to live in poverty, although that talent cannot be measured on paper or in a classroom. Even within the realm of reading, writing, and 'rithmetic, skills diverge. A brilliant mathematical theorist may be unable to count money reliably enough to work as a cashier. Since skills and contributions come in so many dimensions, any system that tries to reward merit cannot help but do considerable injustice.

The same applies to good and bad behavior. Some people, for instance, feel that it is better to have a fist fight than it is to cover a grudge in layers of verbal hostility that preserve it for a lifetime. Some people regard it as damaging and hypocritical to hide their anger behind a polite smile, or behind the trappings of giving due process to someone they represent. It is apparent that both legislation and law enforcement are quite arbitrary about defining degrees of impropriety, so that even killing can be accepted or demanded, as it is with soldiers in combat. It is also obvious that, if politics could be dispensed with, enforcement even of existing law could show the rich to be far more seriously crooked than the poor; and what is arguably lawful is not necessarily virtuous. The law, for example, allows one to be perfectly selfish while being perfectly law abiding.

All in all, there is good reason to suppose that the poor cope with poverty and one another as well as the rich do with wealth and the wealthy. Honesty and virtue are not implied by social success, as the record of many a ruthless entrepreneur attests. If the poor behave no worse than the more affluent, then their greater liability to law enforcement and punishment is unjust. [The issue of v hether rich and poor are equal before the law will be discussed in a later chapter.] The behavior of the poor does not merit harsher treatment than does the behavior of other Americans.

In his presidential address to the American Sociological Society in 1939, Edwin Sutherland made a startling assertion: If in fact the poor are no more crooked than the rich, virtually every theory of why people commit crime and of what it takes to stop them loses empirical foundation.

Consider the implications: the disproportionate number of poor prisoners no longer suggest that people are born criminal. Hence, no attempt at eugenics (i.e. sterilizing welfare mothers) will reduce the level of crime in society. Nor can vitamin deficiencies or hormonal imbalances among identified offenders be presumed to imply that nutritional or medical therapy or surgery will cure criminality, except perhaps in isolated cases.

Many mistakenly believe from looking only at the offenders who get caught and punished that crime is associated with characteristics of the poor: failure of parents to teach skills or discipline necessary for good school performance; failure to have two parents at home; having an alcoholic or criminal parent; hanging out with other offenders; or having only blocked opportunities to wealth and security. Social programs designed to meet these problems, like foster care, recreation centers, housing relocation or special school curricula divert attention from the illegalities and other problems shared by more prosperous offenders, who are taught that their crimes and other shortcomings will be ignored and tolerated. If punishment and treatment are based on a false equation of crime and poverty, they neither aid the poor nor control the affluent. Criminal justice that operates on the premise that criminals are poor teaches the very principle that it is supposed to oppose: Might makes right.

On the other hand, this kind of criminal justice may be very effective at social control of another kind. As Canadian legal historian Douglas Hay proposed for English criminal justice of the eighteenth century, law enforcement here may play a significant role in legitimizing a political system that allows the rich to get richer while the poor get prison. From booking of the arrested suspect through booking out of prison (or, once again, in sporadic execution ceremonies), meticulous and elaborate rituals are gone through to demonstrate that the state represents law and order. The meting out of punishment can be highly selective and restrictive as long as it is occasionally impressive, even awesome. Prolonged trials in a magnanimous state seem to give even the "lowest" and "vilest" every opportunity to plead for vindication or mercy. If through such a process the poor get prison, society assumes they deserve it. The American government thus becomes a manifestation of justice itself; both the American political economy and political institutions are redeemed.

As a result, Americans are hardly prone to change the system. "Perhaps government works imperfectly, but who could conceivably design a better one?" This political fatalism leads to a series of rationalizations: "The crime problem is so serious that officials need all the support we can give them." "How can the poor expect government to do more for them when they keep breaking the law?" "If the poor can display so much contempt for law and order, perhaps it shows that they have been overly spoiled by a generous state." "At any rate, our taxes are doing all that can be done to deal with poverty; we might as well get on about our business." "You do not see us in jail; our behavior must be above reproach; there is no call for us to extend ourselves further to participate in social change."

Thus, the belief that criminals are poor breeds sanctimony among officials and more affluent citizens alike.

Criminologists who broach the subject of compassion for offenders regularly hear from officials and from students, "I've never committed a crime," as though to suggest, "If I am pure, why should I have sympathy for criminals?" Most Americans identify themselves as mid-

42

dle class, and criminality is only one of a number of sins and failings middle class folk attribute to the poor, who are also presumed to be dirty, violent, slothful, and dumb. The feeling that "they," the poor, are incapable of rising to respectability goes with the thought that the middle class is incapable of descending to the poor's level. Even if someone in the middle class ends up in criminal court, there is a tendency for judge and jury to believe that the defendant is not really a criminal, but merely a good citizen who happens to have made a mistake.

It has been noted that a class bias is at least partially written into criminal law. But read in another light, penal law does embody an egalitarian spirit. By restricting the power of government, law implies that being bigger or stronger does not justify appropriating lives, liberties, or property from the weaker members of society. The faith that people can be trusted with a government of limited powers is created by the view that civilized members of a society generally share control of scarce resources with others in a fair way, and that one reason people join together in a political system is to pool their resources to obtain greater abundance together than they could individually. In other words, it is in everybody's enlightened self-interest to share resources and to cooperate in using them to meet one another's needs and interests.

Implicit in saying, "I've never committed a crime," is a declaration that one need not share resources with those who have ever done wrong. The statement is representative of a larger meanness of spirit, in which one presumes that others have to earn the right to share resources one controls, rather than presuming that all people have this right as part of their humanity. This meanness of spirit is reflected in many facets of the everyday lives of middle class Americans.

By world standards, Americans pay very low taxes, and

yet many taxpayers believe that the government takes too much of the income that "belongs" to them. Progressive taxation is anathema to many who believe that people with income have earned it. If one can afford to send one's children to private school, or if one has no children, then many believe that one should pay less of a tax burden to support public schooling for others. If labor is cheap elsewhere, many believe that those who earn profits from a business have no duty to keep a plant open to provide employment to a community. When money becomes scarce in an enterprise, those with seniority believe that they have a right to cast off junior co-workers or demand the greatest pay concessions from the lowest level rather than sacrificing some of their own income for the common good. It is deemed inappropriate for senior managers to share information that only they can understand and use properly, a feeling that extends to many levels of social service workers' treatment of clients or patients. People who own their own cars should not be expected to subsidize public transport. If one invests money in renovating property in the inner city, one has every right to expect that property values in the surrounding neighborhood will rise until the poor can no longer afford to pay their rent. If aging parents grow to be unable to care for themselves, they have no right to expect their children to rearrange their lives to care for them. The list of examples could go on and on.

In deciding what is mine and not yours to share, we are virtually consumed by formal paraphernalia for establishing the criteria by which some will be privileged to enjoy wealth and power, and some others won't. Just as judgments of criminal courts draw lines between the deserving and the undeserving, so grades, degrees, test scores, closed personnel reviews, resumes, and any number of other indices are used to decide what people

are qualified to share of the resources we control. By using such devices, we literally make our might right. In
this respect, literal violation of the law aside, Americans
routinely violate the grander spirit of the law.

The petty nature of the offenses of many inmates can
contrast strikingly with the hurt law-abiding citizens
routinely cause. Hard workers who offend their seniors
are often fired, in some cases because their work
represents at least an implicit rejection of the methods
on which the seniors have staked their reputations. Often
the harshest critics make a point of smiling encouragement in face-to-face confrontation; they offend as stealth-
ily as the professional burglar.

In some fields fining and layoffs end careers of persons
who have worked for years at distinguishing themselves.
By contrast, the damage done by stealing a television set
pales to insignificance. The burglar is expected to show
remorse; the business superiors are left with a sense of
rectitude for upholding standards that often, by their own
admission, they themselves could not meet.

All kinds of viciousness go on regularly. Intrigue and
infighting abound in the workplace, and they are also common to parents and husbands who arbitrarily ridicule, in-
timidate, abuse, and dictate to family members. It is common for those who "have" to disregard the interests and
concerns of those who "have not." The more affluent
seem to be as prone as the stereotypical poor to do unto
others before they can be done unto, to cause pain with
indifference to well-being of others.

The economic and physical well-being of middle-class
Americans is threatened every bit as much by law-abiding
peers and superiors as by the criminals police identify.
Our persistence in attacking crime by attacking the poor
is rather like taking a single patent medicine to cure all
our aches and pains instead of basing the remedy on a

proper and specific medical diagnosis. Until we recognize that the harm we know as crime permeates the culture of rich and poor alike, the risk that Americans pose to one another's well-being will continue unabated.

"Some groups are more law abiding than others."

I will adopt the regimen which in my best judgment is beneficial to my patients, and not for their injury or for any wrongful purpose.

Hippocratic oath

THERE ARE certain groups in our society that have a reputation for being more law-abiding than others. Statistics will confirm that some groups of people do not commit as many crimes as others. There is, however, a reason for these statistical miscalculations and the public willingness to attribute to some groups high quotients of honesty. Some professionals are in a position to commit crimes that cannot be detected without more effort than law enforcement officials are willing to spend. A good example of this public trust of a profession and its violation involves physicians.

On the average, physicians earn $70,000 a year, more than any other occupational group. The need for additional money at the risk of criminal apprehension would, therefore, seem to be absent.

This chapter was written in collaboration with Henry N. Pontell, assistant professor, Program in Social Ecology, University of California, Irvine.

47

Physicians, however, commit crimes. They split fees, write illegal prescriptions, and perform illegal abortions. They also commit crimes not peculiar to their profession; like other mortals, they lie, they steal, and they kill.

The belief that physicians are more honest than other groups is centuries old, but it was not until the early 1900s that doctors gained official validation as the medicine men of our society. It was then that Congress passed legislation limiting to physicians the prescribing or dispensing of opiates in the conviction that drug addiction would thus be effectively controlled. The hoped-for effect did not occur. Rather, physicians freely dispensed opiates to those people they felt in need of the drugs. Some made large profits by turning their practices into warehouse distribution points.

Medicare and Medicaid

More recently, trust in the medical profession has led to fraud and abuse in medical-benefit programs such as Medicare and Medicaid, and in third-party insurance programs like Blue Cross/Blue Shield. The government was not concerned with fraud and abuse when Medicare and Medicaid were enacted in 1965. President Lyndon Johnson was much more fearful that the medical profession would refuse to treat patients covered under the two programs. The American Medical Association (AMA) opposed enactment of Medicare, believing that access to health care should be based on ability to pay and not simply on age. To pacify AMA members and as a way to encourage them to participate in a program they opposed, early administrators were prone to initiate as few rules and regulations as possible and to dissuade enforcement agents from investigating doctors for fraud. As one enforcement agent put it years later, "We built this giant edifice and failed to put any control into it. We sort of said, 'Come in and take what you want.' "

The public became aware that not all participants in Medicare were behaving honestly when in the late 1970s *Sixty Minutes* reported wholesale distribution of narcotics in Chicago. The expose had immediate consequences. A special task force was appointed by the Illinois Attorney General, and prosecutive and investigative staffs went to work. In addition, the Illinois health department was given a shot of money to establish some sort of controls over the dispensation of moneys to health-care providers. Until that time, physicians merely had to submit bills to be paid; the bills were not even subject to audit.

In the late 1970s, Claude Pepper, chair of the House Committee on Aging, held a series of hearings that led to the enactment of various laws aimed at stemming the fraud and abuse cases then being uncovered with increasing frequency. One physician, it was learned, had been charging the government for treatment of nursing-home patients when, in actuality, he was on vacation in the Bahamas. Some doctors would simply walk through a nursing home saying "Hi" to the patients in their path, count the salutation as a visit to each of them, and bill the government accordingly. A dentist charged the government for removing thirty-two impacted wisdom teeth from one patient because the government paid more for the removal of impacted teeth than it did for pulling normal teeth. An ophthamologist was doing cataract operations on healthy eyes because the government would pay $563 for each eye. At least two psychiatrists were found to have been having sex with patients and charging the government for the pleasure. When one of the "patients" became pregnant and had the child, the doctor kidnapped the baby.

Many of these behaviors are known to exist in clinics, notoriously in New York City, that cater mostly to welfare groups. Various practices go on, including such things as "ganging," "ping-ponging," and providing unnecessary services. Ganging is the term used when a physician treats and bills all members of a family present when only one is actually ill. Ping-ponging is a practice somewhat similar to fee-splitting; physicians simply recommend that the patient go see another physician in the clinic. An ear, nose, and throat man, for example, might send a patient to the ophthalmologist. Such practices tie in with the third area, unnecessary services. It is quite common for a patient upon entering the clinic to be asked to supply blood, urine, or any of a whole host of other bodily fluids for testing without ever having seen a physician.

The poor, disabled, and elderly are particularly vulnerable to unnecessary treatments. It is not uncommon for interns practicing in large general hospitals to educate themselves on such people through experiments or useless surgery. Their behavior in these matters is quite similar to street criminals. When a physician admits a patient to a hospital long before it is necessary, the physician is in effect, and literally, kidnapping the patient. Physicians also commit a form of extortion. A patient who disagrees with an MD or asks too many questions will simply be urged to find another physician. Worse, once in the hospital, the physician will argue that the patient who does not agree with the treatment may leave. The patient, of course, has no such ability.

Comparatively few doctors are guilty of gross behavior such as this. Most of us would feel that our own doctors do not engage in any of them, with the exception perhaps of unnecessary procedures. That is also the feeling of most enforcement agents. On the other hand, most agents are convinced that doctors are nickel-and-diming the program. That is, they order an unnecessary test here and there or perhaps upgrade a procedure. Upgrading occurs when a physician does one service and charges for one slightly more expensive. As one high-ranking enforcement official put it, "If we took all the crooks and put them on a ship, the programs would still go broke, because it's the small amounts that are really killing us."

Current minimum estimates of the losses due to medical fraud and abuse are 10 percent of the health-care dollars paid by third-party programs—more than $7 billion in losses on the government's side, and more than $6 billion for Blue Cross and Blue Shield alone.

Physicians and other health-care providers stole more money last year than all the robbers, burglars, and other assorted thieves responsible for crime on the street.

Causes

Why do doctors commit crime? Why do doctors, one of the most prestigious groups in society, abuse and defraud medical programs?

The position of the medical profession is that there are a few "bad apples," and that these "bad apples" commit crime out of greed. Take, for example, drugs. Many of the drugs that are sold on the street were prescribed by doctors originally. Some doctors, a few, freely give out prescriptions; enforcement agents believe that some give out thousands a day. If one puts the cost at ten dollars for each office visit, thousands of prescriptions add up to tens of thousands of dollars. The American Medical Association says, "Throw these people in jail." The agents, argues the AMA, should go after crooked doctors.

At the other end of the spectrum are those people who argue that all physicians occasionally steal. That is, every doctor will upgrade a service, order an unnecessary procedure, or perhaps bill for something he did not do. People who hold this position say that the fee-for-service nature of medical care provides a fiscal incentive for such behavior; the more the physician does, or says is done, the more he or she makes.

Once again, take the example of drugs that reach the streets. The AMA admits that not all prescription drugs on the street come from "bad apples." Some doctors, it argues, need education about when to limit the use of drugs, and others are duped by patients faking ailments to obtain drugs. Finally, the AMA says that some doctors are in need of rehabilitation. The medical profession is notorious for drug abuse among its members; the percentage of addicts is far higher among doctors than among members of any other profession.

Many critics, however, tend to blame the fee-for-service system itself. A different payment mechanism would have different results. Take an example. Health maintenance organizations (HMOs) care for an individual's yearly health-care needs at a fixed rate and hire physicians on fixed salaries to care for a number of patients. Under such a system, there is a fiscal incentive to undertreat. Once again, using drugs as an example: the crooked doctor with a greedy heart would not write prescriptions because he would receive no extra remuneration for writing them. Crooked doctors, in fact, would be likely to undertreat a patient. The doctor who needed an education, who overprescribed simply out of ignorance, would have a strong incentive not to waste energy and time obtaining that education. Duped doctors would be less likely to prescribe drugs; they might not let themselves be so easily fooled if they saw their own time, and hence money, being spent to finance the habits of addicts. Finally there is little that could be done with those physicians who need rehabilitation. Adoption of the HMO concept could not possibly affect their abuse of drugs other than to make them pay for their own habits.

Health maintenance organizations are gaining in popularity. Blue Cross/Blue Shield, for example, has been buying into HMOs in order to lower costs. California's Medicaid system has gone to a health-maintenance arrangement in which contracts are negotiated with hospitals to care for all the indigents in an area. Greatly reduced costs are expected.

The issue, of course, is not as clear cut as the above discussion implies. There are myriad reasons why individuals commit certain behaviors. Physicians' dissatisfaction with government repayment, for example, is often alleged to contribute to fraud and abuse. The government normally pays about one half of what a doctor would receive from a private patient; so the physician may feel it necessary to overcharge the government to make back "legitimate" costs. Some doctors argue that they would not be able to continue their practice in indigent areas if forced to comply with government regulations, that they cheat in order to supply medical services where there would otherwise be none.

The medical profession also argues that government regulations are confusing and unnecessary. This position is not unwarranted. Health and Human Services, for example, recently promulgated a summary of laws and practices in various states in which a practice was applauded in one state and condemned in other states. Additional paper work, rules, and inadequate reimbursement are all factors which, physicians argue, contribute to fraud and abuse.

Enforcement agents are faced with a formidable task, indeed. Consider the following three issues:

First, those charged with enforcing the law must

develop tactics to combat the expertise of the doctors. How does one prove a procedure was unnecessary? The agents find that one physician is doing ten times the number of procedures that similar physicians in the same vicinity are using. Such evidence, however, is not proof of criminal intent. To prove fraud, the agents must show that the individual doctor intended to defraud. How does one prove that the doctor intended to defraud and was not being extra careful out of concern for patients?

Second, removal of a physician from a practice may leave a group of innocent people without medical assistance. Many areas may be served by only one doctor, and the fact that a physician acts criminally does not necessarily mean that other services are dispensable.

Third, it is difficult to obtain a conviction. A physician is usually able to hire the best lawyers in town and will most likely be of a similar economic background as the prosecutor or judge who must weigh the evidence. The doctor will be better able to cast shady actions in a decent light than the average criminal. Convincing a judge or jury that the physician is guilty of a crime and deserves punishment is not easy.

Notwithstanding these difficulties, some efforts are being made to control medical fraud. At the federal level, Congress established the Office of Inspector General (OIG) in 1976 to help get rid of the growing amount of fraud, waste, and abuse that is recognized to exist in the Department of Health and Human Services. Up until that time, investigations had been handled within the Health Care Financing Administration. The introduction of the OIG created a separate unit, originally intended to handle criminal investigations of fraud committed by health-care professionals as well as others involved in Health and Human Service projects. Subsequently, however, the agency switched its emphasis from criminal investigation to auditing and management analysis. As one publication out of the OIG office explains, "The OIG provides information to the policy-makers so that the policies they promulgate create an environment wherein dollars are expended for necessary services and channelled in the most effective manner possible."

Although the new goals of the OIG sound laudable, to a large extent they reflect the inability of the office to obtain criminal convictions against health-care providers. Enforcement officials have proved much more effective at obtaining civil and administrative penalties. In the past five years, 329 health care providers and professionals have been barred from Medicare program participation. Under this procedure, the physician or other provider is banned from billing Medicare for services over a specified time period, normally less than five years. Another new piece of legislation aimed at avoiding the problems associated with criminal prosecution is the Civil Money Penalties Law, signed by Ronald Reagan on August 13, 1981, which allows the OIG to proceed with a civil case rather than a criminal one. It is much easier to prove a violation civilly than it is to prove criminal liability. The new Civil Money Penalty, if implemented, will allow the errant professional to be fined up to $2,000 for each improper claim and an additional assessment of up to twice the fraudulently claimed amount in addition to any suspension from Medicare or Medicaid that may be imposed. Such laws, however, ensure that fewer and fewer cases will be handled criminally.

Individual states have begun to initiate efforts to control fraud and abuse in their Medicaid programs, usually at the request of the federal government. In 1976, besides starting the Office of Inspector General, Congress authorized federal funding (90 percent of the costs for the first three years, 75 percent thereafter) to establish state fraud units. The purpose of these units, as defined by Congress, was to ferret out, investigate, and prosecute the fraud that normal law enforcement officials do not have the expertise to deal with.

The fastest growing area for control of fraud and abuse by health-care professionals is in the private sector. Such carriers as Blue Cross/Blue Shield, Aetna, and Prudential are concerned about fraud because it drains potential earnings. General Motors, for example, pays more money to Blue Cross/Blue Shield than it does to U.S. Steel. Ford adds $400 to the cost of every car and truck for health-care insurance. These large corporations demand that their insurance carrier do something to hold down the cost of premiums. When estimates of health-care fraud and abuse run between 10 and 25 percent of the private insurance bill, it is not surprising that companies work to minimize losses.

Rising costs have greatly reduced the fervor that existed in this country merely two decades ago to provide equal health care for all. The truth is, the astronomical growth in expenses has been accompanied by little improvement in overall health. The United States, for example, still ranks twelfth among western countries in infant mortality rates. Moreover, concern over costs has turned corporations against their previous allies, the medical profession. Corporations had been concerned that an unhealthy workforce was an unproductive workforce, so money spent on improved health care seemed a good investment. Costs today, however, are so high as to make the investment increasingly unattractive.

It should not be surprising, therefore, that both private and government sectors are turning to new models like HMOs. HMOs, by offering a built-in incentive to undertreat, will not eliminate criminal behavior. They will, however, undoubtedly change its form. One technique, for example, used by crooked HMOs is to send an individual into a largely indigent area prior to any sign-up of members. Posing as a health inspector, the individual goes from residence to residence conducting health surveys. Households that show a high probability of illness are passed over when it comes sign-up time, thereby ensuring larger profits.

The model is yet to be invented that will do away totally with fraud and abuse in the medical profession, or any other. No matter how high their prestige, incomes, or education, all groups are vulnerable to criminal activity by its members.

MYTH FOUR

"White-collar crime is nonviolent."

With America's prisons bulging—a record 412,303 people are doing time in state and federal prisons today, double the number just a decade ago—it's hard enough to find cell space for the violent criminals from whom society must be protected.

John Jenkins, The Ambassador Magazine of TWA

WHITE-COLLAR CRIME is violent crime.

There is a common belief shared by the general public and criminal-justice personnel that white-collar crime is only economic. That is, "crime in the suites" involves money being taken from a group rather than some physical attack on a victim. The treatment of white-collar crime as economic, nonviolent crime is clearly evidenced in statements by high Reagan administration officials who have defined white-collar crime and violent crime as two mutually exclusive behaviors. Attorney General William F. Smith said in regard to Reagan's policy on crime, "Top priority... would be violent crime. That would be closely followed by organized crime, by drug enforcement, and by white-collar crime in due course." Smith's ranking of crime priorities seems to say that white-collar crime lacks a violent component, a position unsupported by the evidence.

Drug Companies

One major area prone to violent white-collar crime is the pharmaceutical industry. Parke-Davis, for example, manufactures an antibiotic known as Chloromycetin which was widely sold in the 1950s and 1960s. Salesmen for the company urged physicians to use the antibiotic for patients with everything from minor colds, flus, and ear infections, to more rare diseases. They didn't tell doctors that the drug causes aplastic anemia in approximately one out of 30,000 people. The odds of getting aplastic anemia are slight, but the results are fatal. In the 1960s Chloromycetin was being given to millions of people, killing several people each year.

The fact that Chloromycetin killed people was known in the early 1950s. Warnings were published in medical journals and on the drug package itself, but the danger was generally poorly communicated or ignored. Although Parke-Davis was never taken to criminal court, it was held to be civilly liable for many deaths.

An unfortunate aspect of those deaths was that the drug probably would not have helped the victims. Antibiotics are often given where the chances are slim that they will actually alleviate the illness because most doctors believe that patients want some kind of medicine. Tetracyclene, an antibiotic prescribed for even such minor "ailments" as acne, fills a similar function for doctors today. Parke-Davis's salesmen's claims that Chloromycetin was a cure-all, combined with the physicians' desires to give their patients something, assured that Chloromycetin would be widely used despite its danger.

Park-Davis is not the only pharmaceutical company to have misled the public and officials regarding their products. Richardson-Merrill has been involved in at least two drug related cover-ups. The first involved MER-29, a drug widely marketed and reported to reduce cholesterol levels. Some people who took the drug got cataracts and experienced loss or thinning of hair. A former employee of Richardson-Merrill, a maintenance worker named Beulah, came forward and informed the Federal Drug Administration that Richardson-Merrill lied about test results. She told the FDA that when monkeys died during the testing of MER-29, they were replaced with healthy monkeys. Richardson-Merrill was found liable and fined $80,000: the equivalent of a twenty-dollar traffic ticket for someone earning $20,000 a year, and obviously insufficient to deter the firm from future illegal behavior. Recently, it has been found civilly liable in a case involving birth defects linked to the use of one of its products—Bendectine. Bendectine is prescribed for morning sickness during pregnancy, but is of questionable value.

In actuality, Richardson-Merrill is quite lucky to be in business. In the early 1960s it was the United States distributor for Thalidomide, an English product that the FDA would not allow to be marketed in the U.S. pending further tests. Richardson-Merrill, however, gave the drug to physicians and urged them to prescribe it for their patients in hope of speeding along the testing process. Thalidomide caused scores of horrible birth defects, and was quickly removed from the English market. The FDA's early decision not to allow immediate sale of the drug prevented many birth defects in the United States and saved Richardson-Merrill from suits that would have undoubtedly destroyed the company.

The health-care industry is particularly susceptible to violent behaviors, and hospitals present an especially good example. Physicians practicing in hospitals maim and kill thousands each year. A study using Teamster members estimates that 10,000 lives are lost each year due to unnecessary surgeries. The union decided to require a second medical opinion before allowing elective surgeries for its members—a move designed to lower costs. Previously, an elective surgery could be done following the advice of one doctor. The inclusion of a second opinion greatly reduced the number of elective surgeries; and it also lowered the amount of deaths.

Another 20,000 lives are lost annually in hospitals due to errors in the prescribing of drugs. Some of these deaths can be attributed to the consequences of different drugs prescribed and taken in combination, others to drugs prescribed without prior testing of the individual patient's susceptibility to potentially lethal side effects. The estimate of 20,000 lives lost was derived in a study of several hospitals in which the records of former patients were reviewed and the percentage of those determined to have died as a result of prescription errors was generalized to national patient loads.

Another 20,000 lives are estimated to be lost due to doctors spreading diseases in hospitals. Researchers studied doctors' practices in hospital emergency rooms and found that doctors would often go from one patient to the next without washing or in other ways sterilizing themselves.

These estimates of lives lost, however, are a minimum figure to attribute to physicians and other health-care providers in that they do not include any lives lost outside the hospital structure. Dentists, for example, are employing general anesthesia, such as sodium pentathol, more and more, making a visit to the dentist as dangerous as many operations. (Most deaths in surgeries are due to the anesthesia.)

Executives of Ford Motor Company knew prior to production of the Pinto that it was particularly susceptible to explosion in a rear-end collision. An inter-office memo revealed that an eight-dollar part would greatly reduce the risk, but recommended waiting until 1976 to add the part in order to save $20 million. The Ford Motor Company was also involved in a case involving automatic transmissions that slipped into reverse. At first, the company denied the existence of the problem, but when continued evidence showed that it indeed did exist, put the blame on consumers, arguing that drivers failed to place the cars properly in the parking gear when they left them unattended. Finally, it was shown that the vehicle did indeed slip into reverse, and not because of driver negligence. Ford, however, was able to minimize its loss, negotiating an agreement with the Reagan administration that required the company merely to place warning placards inside the affected vehicles.

Other parts of the auto industry have also been involved in violent white-collar crime. Firestone, for example, produced a tire which would explode during normal use. B.F. Goodrich was involved in a similar incident, lying about test results of a brake they were producing for fighter jets.

No industry seems safe from the type of behavior that leads to violent outcomes. For example, the Purina Company has been involved in leaking gas into sewer systems causing several Louisville streets to explode one morning. A short time later, the streets would have been crowded and many lives would have been lost.

Conclusions

It is unfortunate but reasonable to assume that the Reagan administration's working definition of white-collar crime will preclude any consideration of possible enforcement alternatives for violent white-collar offenses. The importance of such considerations, however, cannot be underestimated.

Violent white-collar crimes, as all illegalities, can be broken into two areas. The first are crimes of *commission* (the offenders do something they should not have done). The earlier example of a physician performing an unneeded surgery is illustrative. The second are crimes of *omission* (the criminals fail to do something they were required to do). An example would be not ensuring the safety of equipment on a work site. The interesting consideration for those studying violent white-collar crime is that different payment mechanisms lead to different criminal behaviors—ones of omission or ones of commission. In particular, fee-for-service leads to crimes of commission. Fee-for-completed job leads to offenses of omission.

The fee-for-service mechanism requires that the individual pay for each service rendered. A patient, for example, will normally be billed separately for each medical procedure, providing the physician or health-care facility with a fiscal incentive to overtreat. The more procedures one prescribes the more money one makes.

Although some physicians may charge for services never rendered, this is the rarer case, for it is easier for the offender to rationalize overtreatment. What constitutes proper medical treatment is obscured by an overabundance of gray areas. One physician notes, "If a surgeon removes only 20 percent normal appendices, we'd say he is doing a reasonably good job. But if 50 percent are normal, then his surgical judgment is open to question." Such a wide variation about what is proper grants great discretion to the physician, and an accompanying license to do wrongs. On the other hand, it is not easy to clear one's conscience of charging for services never rendered. A second reason to assume that under-treatment is rarer is that overtreatment is not easily recognized. Once a procedure has been performed, it is difficult to prove that it was not needed.

The fee-for-completed job mechanism requires that the consumer purchase an entire product. New car buyers, for example, must purchase complete automobiles even if they want cars without tires (and without the cost of tires). This form of payment provides a fiscal incentive to undertreat. The less cost needed to complete the product, the higher the profit.

Coal mining, for example, is a very dangerous occupation. Over the last forty years, however, it has been made much safer for a number of reasons; two of the more obvious are technological advances and strip mining. Nevertheless, many of the lives saved are caused by increased enforcement regarding safety procedures that have greatly increased the cost of mining coal, and in turn, the cost to the consumer for heat. To judge from the historical record, if left to their own devices, coal mine owners would prefer to scrimp on safety measures in order to increase their profits.

Discussion of the relationship between such things as payment mechanisms and types of criminal behavior can be useful in planning enforcement. The American Medical Association claims lower figures than those cited in this book, but do not disagree that surgeons overtreat. Unneeded treatments are related to a number of factors such as an excess of surgeons and increased technology. The fee-for-service mechanism, however, is the bottom line. Health maintenance organizations decrease treatments and cost by not charging for each physician's service, but rather billing for entire health care. The government and private insurance companies may rely increasingly on such organizations to help curb the rising costs of medical care.

Enforcement agents should be made aware that they will have to deal with different behaviors. That is, fee-for-service leads to overtreatment and billing for services never rendered. Fee-for-complete job, that is, health maintenance organizations, may lead to undertreatment. Ignoring the violent component of white-collar crime guarantees that such distinctions, however, will not be made.

Further, existing situations will not be changed. Recently a delicensed dentist in Kentucky has opened a dental clinic. The ex-dentist does not actually practice dentistry; he hired someone to do that. He lost his license in 1979 after one of his patients died, a four-year-old girl whom he had given a sedative. In addition, he also spent sixteen months in prison for selling drugs, including cocaine. His ownership of the dental clinic, however, violates no laws. The dental commission in Kentucky is reduced to trying to obtain a criminal misdemeanor conviction against the unlicensed dentist on the basis that in realigning a local police officer's dental plate he had illegally practiced. Such ludicrous situations occur because the government fails to make proper consideration of the violent component of white-collar crime. Myths, of course, tend to perpetuate the absurd.

MYTH FIVE

"Regulatory agencies prevent white-collar crime."

Stiff civil and criminal penalties are provided for willful violations of standards. Individual directors, officers, and agents of manufacturers are subject to fines and imprisonment for failing to comply with standards. In addition, consumers may bring suits for damages against violators, and consumer organizations and other private groups may seek court enforcement of product safety standards.

Description of the Consumer Product Safety Act by the Editorial Staff of the Bureau of National Affairs, Inc.

REGULATORY AGENCIES are commonly believed to protect consumers from the abuses and unethical practices of businesses. Almost all sanctions issued against corporations are done so by regulatory agencies, and many take it for granted that these sanctions prevent corporate wrongdoing.

There is some evidence to justify this belief. Take, for example, the National Highway Transportation Safety Act, which allows the National Highway Transportation Board to recall defective automobiles. Prior to the Reagan administration the Board was ordering a growing number of recalls, in 1977 citing eighteen million cars as poten-

66

tially hazardous. Such recalls are expensive for auto manufacturers and the agency's success in effecting them would seem to show that customers' rights can be protected by regulation.

Regulatory agencies, however, usually can do very little to protect consumers against corporate greed. To understand why, it's necessary to review briefly the history of regulation.

Fairplay Through Competition

The first regulatory agency, the Interstate Commerce Commission (ICC) was established in the late 1800s in reaction to the growing number and power of corporate trusts in America. Classical capitalistic economists had believed with Adam Smith that a large number of small competing firms was the best guarantee of ethical behavior. Smith himself theorized that large establishments with absentee owners, such as corporations, would not be guided by honest feelings. To one of his persuasion, regulation was anathema. Government interference in the marketplace could only lead to inequities, it was presumed, and any legislation to control the marketplace, no matter how well intentioned, would always be manipulated to benefit those who could influence the final form of the regulation. Once having gained the upper hand, the powerful would use it to get more and more power in an ever increasing spiral.

In the early and mid 1800s, the United States followed a laissez-faire policy toward business. Legislatures were inclined not to pass any type of regulation dealing with business, listening to entrepreneurs of the time who argued that the best form of regulation was none at all. By the late 1800s, however, there was a growing public

67

concern. Businesses were no longer the small entities that Adam Smith had talked about, and many companies were combining in a loose fashion called trusts. A sugar trust, for example, is a combination of sugar manufacturers who set uniform prices, stopping free market competition and, in effect, giving the public an ultimatum: Buy at this price or not at all. There was also mounting concern with what appeared to be escalating power on the part of some individual companies. Rockefeller, for example, was able to obtain rate discounts from the railroads for shipping oil because he was their largest customer. These discounts enabled him to charge less for oil, which in turn enabled him to undercut his competitors until they went bankrupt. All told, such tactics enabled the large Rockefeller interests to grow even larger and ultimately gain monopolistic control of the oil industry.

Corporate leaders were not deaf to the public clamor for reform. Revolution was not an unheard-of idea and some capitalists were seriously worried that socialists might take over. Corporate leaders suggested that it would be better to enact legislation—their own legislation—rather than have some other type forced down their throats. Richard S. Olney, a railroad attorney who became Attorney General under President Grover Cleveland, wrote the president of the Burlington Railroad in 1882 outlining ideas on the Interstate Commerce Comission. It "can be of great use to the railroads. It satisfies the popular clamor for government supervision of railroads, at the same time that supervision is almost entirely minimal. The part of wisdom is not to destroy the commission, but to utilize it." And in a similar vein, Samuel Insull is quoted as saying in regard to regulation, it is better to "help shape the right kind of regulation, than to have the wrong kind forced upon you."

It is not surprising to learn that most regulatory laws

are, for the most part, written by business people. The Federal Trade Commission Act, for example, differs little from legislation proposed by the National Civic Federation, a group consisting mostly of corporate businessmen.

The main point to be made in regard to the historic development of regulatory agencies is that they are in response to public recognition of a problem. Lacking public clamor, government did little to try to change the situation. Once the public began to urge some solution, however, corporate leaders stepped in to shape the form of legislation that eventually regulated their behavior.

Regulatory Agencies

The basic structure of regulatory agencies favored by business leaders requires a diffusion of power. For example, the Federal Trade Commission has five commissioners who are appointed by the president and confirmed by the Senate. There is a stipulation that no more than three commissioners can be of the same political party. With few exceptions—notably the Environmental Protection Agency, which is governed by a single administration—most regulatory agencies are similarly structured. They are under few other legislative restraints, however, and establish their own rules.

By and large, they seek non-criminal, non-combative resolutions to problems involving civil and administrative penalties. Administrative penalties can be of various types. For example, an agency may choose to issue a warning to a corporation that it believes or, most of the time, knows to be in violation of the law. The corporation, thus warned, will normally discontinue the practice. Another very common administrative procedure is called a consent decree in which a corporation, without admitting past guilt, agrees not to violate the law in the future without admitting past guilt. Such an agreement allows the corporation to avoid admitting blame that could be used in future civil suits by private citizens. Warnings and consent decrees represent the largest proportion of actions taken by regulatory agencies. Marshall Clinard and Peter Yeager in research for their excellent book, *Corporate Crime*, found that one out of every two sanctions against manufacturing corporations involved either a warning or a consent order.

The administrative procedure of the Federal Trade Commission (FTC) is illustrative of most agencies. The FTC responds mainly to complaints because its caseload is much too large to allow it to search out violations of law. In one case, for example, a business agreed to stop its alleged false advertising in the Seattle area where the case originated. Meanwhile, it continued its practices in southern California without the FTC's knowledge.

Letters of complaints are first forwarded to the proper FTC staff members, who decide whether to take action or to let the matter drop. If, following an investigation, the staff members feel that the commission should act, they draw up a complaint document. If the commission then decides to issue the complaint, a copy is first sent to the party named who can then sign a cease-and-desist order without admitting any violation of the law. If no agreement is reached, the commission may then issue the formal complaint and set a hearing date.

The respondent can choose to contest the complaint, first in a preliminary hearing before a trial examiner and then an appeal to the commission for an oral hearing. Both the hearing before the trial examiner and before the commissioners are similar to civil court proceedings.

If the commission also rules against the respondent, it issues a cease-and-desist order. The corporation may also

70

be required to take remedial action such as refunds, replacements, or damages paid to the victims.

The defendants, however, may wish to appeal to the United States Court of Appeals, and if necessary, to the United States Supreme Court. As in cases that reach the appeals courts through lower civil or criminal courts, the FTC decision is usually overturned only on points of law—not on facts.

If the respondent loses and fails to follow the cease-and-desist order, he may be either fined or found to be in criminal contempt of court. Current case law limits the sanction for criminal contempt. In a case involving Paul T. Cheff, president of the Holland Furnace Company, the United States Supreme Court in 1966 effectively limited FTC punishments to corporate executives. The case is worth studying for its implications.

For thirty years the Holland Furnace Company used what is known as "tear and scare" tactics. Salesmen would go to the homes of individuals, especially elderly people, in winter posing as safety inspectors. The "safety inspectors" would express concern over the existing furnace, and later different salesmen would go to these homes to sell new furnaces. Usually the cost of the furnace was far in excess of what could be bought elsewhere, and of lower quality. Holland was selling 1920-type coal burners in the 1950s.

The FTC first acquired a stipulation from Holland that it would stop these practices because they were misleading, but Holland didn't stop. Four years passed between the original complaint (1954) and the FTC cease-and-desist order (1958). During that time the commission compiled ten thousand pages of testimony about the Holland Company from all over the country. The company appealed the cease-and-desist order and lost, but still failed to comply. In 1962 the FTC filed a petition to cite for criminal contempt of court and finally, in 1965 the Appeals Court sentenced the company to a fine of $100,000. Two former sales managers were fined $500 each. Paul T. Cheff, the president of the company, was given a six-month jail sentence. The company and the president petitioned the Supreme Court which declined to review the case of the company, but granted a review in the case of the president. On June 6, 1966 the Supreme Court held that Cheff's conviction and sentencing was valid, but in doing so the Court held that six months was the maximum sentence permissible for criminal contempt.

Cheff, however, did not serve six months. He served two months, and then was paroled. Senator Warren G. Magnuson later noted that at one time Holland Furnace had cost the American public thirty million dollars a year.

The FTC is not alone in its inability to punish corporate violators swiftly and effectively; most regulatory agencies are in the same boat. A case involving Beech Aircraft and the Federal Aviation Administration (FAA) is illustrative. In the 1960s, Beech Aircraft knowingly produced airplanes with faulty fuel tanks. When the planes' gas tanks were less than half full, they experienced a loss of power when the gas in the tank was sloped away from the import valves. Air was sucked into the fuel lines and injected into the engines, which would then die. The faulty tanks caused several crashes and the loss of many lives.

A civil court found Beech liable for the deaths, and in one case a Santa Ana, California jury awarded the survivors of victims over $27 million. In that case, the pilot took off in a twin engine Beech plane and, as the plane started its climb, one of the engines quit, causing the engine on the other side to make an abrupt movement forward, sloshing the fuel away from the import valve. The pilot, trying to start one engine, was soon faced with the other quitting. Even if he had been able to start one of the engines, it would have only caused another abrupt move, which would have sloshed the fuel away from the import valve again. A crash was inevitable.

Inneroffice memoranda clearly indicate that Beech Aircraft was well aware of the problem in 1961. Unsuccessful early efforts were made to correct the problem by install- ing baffles in the fuel tanks. Beech then sent warning let- ters. Unfortunately, only the owners of single-engine planes were notified, although the danger existed with twin-engine planes as well.

Following the finding of civil fault in 1971, the Federal Aviation Administration ordered Beech Aircraft to install placards in each of the planes, notifying the pilot that take- offs should not be made with less than a half-full tank. The FAA added the stipulation that if the problem was solved in an airplane, the placard could be removed. Beech immediately produced a fuel tank that solved the problem which they would install at the owner's expense, and thus enable the owner to remove the placard. The order to put the placard in the planes was the only sanction imposed by the Federal Aviation Administration for this neglect of human safety, which involved several violations of FAA rules and death.

How was Beech able to hide this blatant problem from the Federal Aviation Administration for so long? It was able to because the FAA relies on aircraft manufacturers to report any problems with their own planes.

Factors That Limit Enforcement

Several factors combine to limit the enforcement abilities of regulatory agencies, the most commonly cited constraint being budget. In the judgement of academics who study regulatory agencies, regulatory officials, and

73

enforcement agents, the inadequate budget makes the agencies unable to seek out violations. This has a profound impact on enforcement because most white-collar crimes are not recognized by the victim. An individual, for example, who has been sold an unnecessary repair on his automobile is unlikely to realize that he has been victimized. Similarly, a person who pays a penny or two more for a product because several manufacturers have conspired to fix prices is unaware of such collusion.

Even when a regulatory agency believes that a crime is committed, budget constraints limit effective enforcement. Corporations are capable of hiring the best defense possible while regulatory agencies must rely on the minimal resources afforded by Congress. Clinard and Yeager report that the Security Exchange Commission, the National Highway Transportation Safety Administration, and the Consumer Products Safety Administration have combined enforcement budgets of $20 million or less, and that these budgets must pay for all help. Corporations have much larger budgets to spend on their defense; happily for them, such costs often are tax deductible.

Another constraint on the sanctioning ability of regulatory agencies derives from limitations placed on them by legislatures. Laws are often written to limit the ability of regulatory agencies to do anything meaningful. The Indiana Consumer Protection Division (CPD), part of the state's Attorney General's Office, is a good example. The division was started in the early 1970s as part of the wave of consumer agencies. The CPD, however, has very little power. Normally, complaints are received over the phone from a consumer. The agency then forwards a complaint form to the consumer. If the consumer returns the complaint form listing the problem, the CPD notifies the business of the complaint. This often will solve the problem for the consumer which stops the case. The agency can only act as a mediator; it may not legally fight the business. If the problem is solved between the business and the consumer, the issue is then dropped by the CPD, leaving other consumers vulnerable to the same abuse. In this manner, the Indiana legislature was able to protect businesses from any meaningful action.

Another problem that exists in regulatory agencies is "turf" conflicts. These arise when two regulatory agencies have jurisdiction over similar areas. The right of both the Federal Trade Commission and the U.S. Justice Department to handle anti-trust cases is one example. Another instance that existed until recently involved two Health and Human Services departments, Health Care Financing Administration and the Office of Inspector General. The Health Care Financing Administration (HCFA) was required to review cases of potential provider fraud and pass suspect cases along to the Office of Inspector General (OIG). For a while, however, cases were not passed along. One of the reasons was that the HCFA had formally handled all of a case including investigation. Jealousy arose when the OIG came into existence and took the investigatory rights away from HCFA. It was also HCFA's belief that the OIG, inexperienced in health issues, was not properly handling the cases. HCFA chose to handle cases within their own office rather than forwarding them. HCFA has substantially less sanctioning ability than the OIG. It may apply administrative sanctions such as recovering lost monies, while the OIG can conduct criminal investigations, which are passed along to a U.S. Attorney General for possible prosecution. Fortunately, the conflict was eased in 1983 when the HCFA people were transferred to the OIG, remedying the situation, one hopes.

Another major factor limiting the enforcement ability of regulatory agencies is the considerable influence of corporations. For example, corporations will lobby with agencies to pass rules of benefit to them. Consumers, lacking any united force, will be outgunned by such efforts. Regulatory agencies, therefore, normally have only business to listen to for advice.

Another example of businesses' influence stems from the "revolving door" policy. For years, companies have chosen to hire the very people who have once regulated them. A Federal Trade Commission attorney, for example, can look forward to a high-paying job with IBM or some other corporation. Such a policy tends to limit the zeal of regulatory officials. They are not prone to bite the hand that will later feed them. Fortunately, recent regulatory agencies such as the Consumer Products Safety Commission have stipulations that an individual may not serve in the industry they have regulated for a stated number of years after leaving the commission. It should be noted, however, that the revolving door policy is a two-way street. That is, regulators not only go to the businesses that they regulate, but business people come to the regulators. Individuals often will take a leave of absence to go and work for a regulator. The agencies welcome such additions as adding to the expertise of their staff.

Corporate influence in limiting sanctioning goes beyond the regulatory agencies. For example, the inadequate budgets mentioned before are the result of corporate lobbying with Congress. Similarly, legal limitations placed on the Indiana Consumer Protection Division are also the handicraft of corporate lobbyists.

One example of corporate influence pressuring Congress to limit regulatory power is apparent with the tobacco industry. As early as 1954 there was published evidence that smoking was linked to lung cancer. The Surgeon General of the United States, acting on the mounting evidence against cigarette smoking, created a committee to study its effects. In 1964 the committee issued a report which stated that "cigarette smoking is a health hazard of sufficient importance in the United States to warrant appropriate remedial action." One week after the committee's report, the FTC issued a notice of proposed rulemaking. The next move was by the tobacco industry. Rather than try to delay the commission's action, the industry attempted to bypass it and succeeded by taking its plea straight to Congress. Congress has the power to change any rule that a regulatory agency may choose to establish or to take the subject out of an agency's hands by passing its own law. Congress's cigarette law required that a much less stringent health warning be placed on cigarette packages than the one the FTC originally proposed. The law also placed a three-year moratorium on regulatory action of the tobacco industry by either the FTC or an individual state.

A similar case involved the Federal Communications Commission (FCC). During the 1960s, the FCC proposed to enact into administrative law the National Association of Broadcasters' code on commercials. The networks decided that such an action would not be to their benefit, and their argument won swift approval in Congress. The House passed a bill saying that the FCC did not have the power to promulgate such a rule and forced the FCC to rescind its action.

Corporations are often able to exercise their influence on the executive branch of government. Though the executive branch can overrule only its own agencies, business often finds ways to use it to affect other agencies as well. One of the most noted cases took place in 1956 when the FTC issued a complaint charging Northfield Mills's Bernard Goldfein, and four others, with violations of the Wool Products Labelling Act and the FTC

Act. The commission alleged that Northfield had been labelling textiles 70 percent guanaco and 30 percent wool when the fabrics contained substantially less than 70 percent guanaco. Northfield eventually negotiated a consent order following the issuance of a cease-and-desist order. The House Subcommittee on Legislative Oversight discovered, however, that Sherman Adams, President Eisenhower's chief White House aide, tried to intervene on behalf of his friend, Goldfein. Adams was forced to resign, but the incident illustrates the influence available to corporations.

The ability of regulatory agencies to enforce laws effectively is further limited by characteristics of the criminal-justice system. Even if a regulatory agency seeks a criminal solution, it is unlikely to obtain a stiff penalty for a number of reasons.

First, prosecutors do not like cases involving corporations. The cases usually are highly complex; millions of pages of transcript are not unheard of. Such massive amounts of evidence make it difficult for the prosecutor to ever fully understand a case. An overworked, underpaid prosecutor finds it much easier to stick to street criminals.

Even a prosecutor who wishes to indict a corporation will probably be outmatched and outgunned by the ability of a corporation to hire the best attorneys. For example, the city of Bloomington, Indiana with a population of 50,000 people, is suing Westinghouse over harmful PCBs that were dumped in sites in the area. Westinghouse, however, has been able to drag the case on for years, simply outlasting incumbent city attorneys.

Another factor weighing in the favor of corporations is that judges are not particularly interested in corporate cases. Just as the case is difficult for the prosecutor to deal with, it is for the judge, too. A judge is not interested in having the calendar clogged for weeks, months or years with a case that may be handled administratively. As stated earler, judges are often of the same social background as those who are standing trial. In fact, corporate offenders may choose to hire the best friend of the judge to defend them—a very common practice.

Further, juries have trouble understanding complex corporate cases. Even when the issues are simple, defense attorneys frequently complicate them with massive amounts of irrelevant information. Under such circumstances, a conscientious jury, faced with the necessity to prove guilt beyond a reasonable doubt in criminal cases, has difficulty coming to a verdict to convict.

These factors, as well as many more, lead to light sentences for corporate offenders. To handle any of their responsibilities, regulatory agencies must utilize administrative sanctions. Warning letters and consent decrees rarely result in media attention, so the public remains unaware of its victimization. Instead of protecting consumers, regulatory agencies shield corporations from public knowledge of their misdeeds.

MYTH SIX

"Rich and poor are equal under the law."

In every particular his (the judge's) conduct should be above reproach. He should be conscientious, studious, thorough, courteous, patient, punctual, just, impartial, fearless of public clamor, regardless of public praise, and indifferent to private political or partisan influences...

Canons of Judicial Ethics
American Bar Association

Some so-called criminals—and I use this word because it's handy, it means nothing to me—I speak of the criminals who get caught as distinguished from the criminals who catch them—some of these so-called criminals are in jail for their first offenses, but nine tenths of you are in jail because you did not have a good lawyer and, of course, you did not have a good lawyer because you did not have enough money to pay a good lawyer. There is no very great danger of a rich man going to jail.

Clarence S. Darrow
Speech to inmates
at Cook Country Jail, 1902

80

THE RICH are as violent and crooked as the poor, so why are they not punished in equal proportion? Why are 48 percent of American prisoners black? Why is it so rare to see rich, prominent people sent to prison? Criminal-justice officials, and indeed many criminologists, say that people are largely punished in proportion to the seriousness and quantity of offenses they commit. How can they believe this?

Looking for Crime

Suppose that most of the officers of an urban police force were to patrol the suites rather than the streets (leaving sufficient cars on the streets to cover emergency calls). Some officers would go through a city hospital's records looking for patterns that suggest unnecessary surgery, and would pursue the suspicion by interviewing patients, their families, and doctors. Doctors who had operated unnecessarily, without informing patients that surgery was elective, might be charged with aggravated assault, or where patients died, with manslaughter. Other officers could go through city records to find improper expenditures by officials, and make arrests for theft. Others might experiment with buying goods and services, finding owners and managers to arrest for fraud. If a high enough proportion of officers did this kind of investigation, those of wealth and position might well be arrested more often than the poor, or if practically all officers did so, the wealthy might even be convicted and punished more often than the poor.

This pattern of enforcement would begin to ensure that the crimes of rich and poor would be detected equally. What makes detection of the crimes of the wealthy harder is that their victims are usually unaware that they've been

81

victimized. How likely is one to discover that surgery was unnecessary? If a firm's unlawful pollution causes one to contract cancer twenty years after, will anyone connect the cause to the effect? If an auto repair service sells a person a part to replace a perfectly good one, how can the customer know that fraud has occurred? Although criminologists have noted that those who commit offenses in private are less likely to come to official notice than those who commit their crimes in the streets, only a few— Stanley Pennington from Indiana University for example—are beginning to notice that even a victim may not detect a crime.

The demonstrated class bias of law enforcement cannot be laid to the personal inadequacies of criminal-justice officials. It would be the rare police officer who would be given time away from patrolling the streets to conduct cumbersome investigations of the rich. Prosecutors are swamped with charges of street crime brought to them by police. The police chief who took officers off the streets, or who even allowed them discretion to do so, would soon be an ex-chief amid public outcry that the streets were being abandoned to the criminal. Law enforcement is essentially an exercise of power over a citizenry; it is literally, inherently political. State politics, or the exercise of state power, will be biased in favor of citizens with more power than others. Short of a violent revolution against people of wealth and position, it is virtually inconceivable that they should be as subject to law enforcement as the poor. Our crime statistics reflect this political reality, and so produce evidence that criminals are poor.

Criminologists' interviews and surveys asking people whether they have committed crimes are part of this skewed evidence. It is laughable to suppose that fraudulent doctors, for instance, would detail false claims for medical insurance on a self-report questionnaire. Instead, self-report surveyors are reduced to asking about more innocuous crimes, to surveying youth more than adults, and to obtaining more confessions from already stigmatized people—like students with poor school records—who have less of a stake in pretending unimpeachable behavior. Outside the realm of criminal justice, citizens are still caught in the political reality that biases them against detecting crimes among higher status persons. But pervasive as the political reality is, it is important to recognize the gap between illegal harm done and the way it is reported.

Even within the realm of street crime, the poor suffer disproportionately from law enforcement. When middle-class parents find children to be trouble at home or at school, they can and do pay for private treatment, or provide tuition to send children to special schools. Parents of lesser means are more likely to have to send their children to juvenile court. Police and youthworkers, and for that matter shopowners, will refer problem children for handling by parents, provided that the parents are "respectable people." Police officers who have worked in many types of neighborhoods acknowledge that they call home to middle-class parents more readily. Between suburban and urban departments, the difference can be even more striking. A department of college-educated officers in a suburb of Minneapolis in the 1970s went so far as to invite parents and children into the station to discuss their problems confidentially, with virtual immunity from formal handling. This is not atypical of suburban forces that political scientist James Q. Wilson describes as having "the service style."

What is true of police is also true of schools. Inner-city schools are more likely than those in wealthier areas to call upon police to patrol there regularly, so that police are more readily available to be called than are parents. Twenty years ago sociologists Aaron Cicourel and John Kitsuse discovered that schools with primarily poor students create a vicious circle. Poor students are expected to do poorly; this stigmatizes them and makes them more prone to cause trouble; this leads school authorities to suppose that they need legal assistance to restore discipline, which further stigmatizes the students; and in the end, this means that these are not the kind of students whom one can afford to indulge as one might indulge someone in trouble in a respectable school full of "good kids." One juvenile court judge said recently that middle-class kids undoubtedly break the law a lot, but somehow she never sees them.

To a significant degree, wealth offers physical opportunity to commit crimes undetected. Children who have access to large recreation rooms with well-stocked bars far enough away from neighboring houses to forestall disturbance can drink underage or use illicit drugs with relative impunity. Those who have only streetcorners to gather at are called "young hoodlums" and are a classic police target. Kids whose parents can buy them cars do not have to steal to cruise. If kids who live in the blighted inner-city travel to more pleasant surroundings for a night on the town, any sign that they "do not belong" in a neighborhood (i.e., having dark skins in a white neighborhood) causes police suspicion. Questioning these kids, or merely following them around, plays into the vicious circle of police/poor citizens relations. Feeling unduly harassed, the youths may well respond hostilely to the police, who then become defensive and try to assert their authority. It is often unclear who strikes the first blow when angry words turn to physical force, but the situation commonly leads to charges of assault on police officers, or of disturbing the peace.

Traffic enforcement presents similar problems. Boredom can induce police to find a pretext to stop cars to check for underage drinking, or for invalid licenses or registrations, especially at otherwise quiet times (and urban police have many of them even at night). Police in many jurisdictions soon learn that stopping people who are too well politically connected causes grief. And, as a matter of professional courtesy, anyone stopped who is identified as a police officer will be let off with a warning at most. In this climate, the stereotype develops that youths, particularly minority youths driving dilapidated cars, are most likely to be driving in violation of the law, both because the bias produces more points against their licenses and because they overwhelmingly are the ones investigated. Police become convinced that efficient law enforcement requires most traffic stops to be of poor youths in dilapidated cars.

In a variety of ways, then, the poor are odds-on favorites to have their violations of law detected.

Court Processing

The bias that pushes poor youths to start accumulating police records is compounded in the courts. When prosecutors decide whether to press formal charges, whether to give those they arrest a break by charging a more minor offense, or whether to accept a plea bargain, a defendant's prior record weighs heavily. Thus a defendant who has begun to accumulate a record is more likely than others to have more serious charges added to the record, and to have the record extended to include formal court findings of guilt. Many criminologists have reported that when prior record and seriousness of charge are held constant, there is little or no racial or class discrimination in the courts. These criminologists overlook the fact that seriousness of offense charged and prior record are products of class discrimination themselves. As the discrimination is compounded, a nineteen-year-old defendant who at age fourteen was first taken into custody for underaged drinking can easily become a "career criminal" who, in the courts' eyes, deserves a maximum term of incarceration. The person already handicapped by poverty who is taken away to jail for a series of minor infractions has less opportunities to become established legitimately in the community, and is more likely to feel the need to associate with "known criminals" and make a livelihood of crime. This is what criminologists call "the labeling effect."

Once taken into custody, wealth and position affect one's chances of obtaining release prior to a court hearing. Prior record, community position of parents (for minors), employment, and, when bail is required, how much cash or assets one can muster to post as security determine whether a person will sleep at home or in jail. With today's crowded courts, those who cannot obtain release prior to juvenile hearing or trial may well have to sit in jail or a detention center for months or even a year, often for longer periods than the sentences they face if tried and convicted. The inducement is strong for defendants in this situation to get to court quickly by pleading guilty to crimes whether they committed them or not. According to criminologist Arye Ratner, those who have begun to accumulate prior records are far more likely than has been recognized to be convicted though innocent. The discrimination in pretrial detention is compounded by the possibility that the police officers, some who cover themselves by lying in court, will be believed and by the ease with which witnesses can be persuaded to misidentify suspects police and prosecutors believe to be guilty. And so the poor are especially likely to accumulate records of criminality even when they have committed no offense.

When conviction has occurred or is likely, the class of the defendant once again plays a role in disposition. For one thing, officials are inclined to believe that "respectable" people are more easily hurt by the mere embarrassment and discomfort of being arrested or charged. Thus, the rich are more likely to be treated as having suffered enough without resorting to incarceration, a situation exemplified by the trial of former Vice President Spiro Agnew. "Good families," good jobs, and other visible contributions of defendants to the community weigh in their favor. It also helps for those who can afford it to show that private arrangements have been made for treatment, or that defendants have continued working without incident while awaiting trial. The poor go to prison by default.

It has been suggested that those who can afford to pay high fees retain better legal counsel than those who have to rely on public defenders. In a way, this is unfair to public defenders, who are often highly experienced and skilled trial lawyers, unlike many private attorneys. On the other hand, money buys time and effort that public defenders with high caseloads cannot afford. Contrast the defender in a large city who carries thirty casefiles to court each morning with the private attorney who can delay proceedings while the client remains free on bail, while expensive depositions are taken from parties to find weaknesses in the prosecution's case, and while experts are retained and character witnesses of high community standing are collected to testify on the defendant's behalf. These opportunities give a considerable edge to the defendant who can afford experienced private counsel. Bear in mind that a first-class defense even of a misdemeanor or traffic offense can cost several thousand dollars.

With discrimination operating in so many ways at so many levels, it is not surprising that officially known offenders and prisoners are overwhelmingly poor even though the rich do citizens more unlawful harm.

Protecting Victims

One rationale offered for being so tough on poor street criminals is that their victims, too, are primarily poor, and need and deserve protection. There are two holes in this line of reasoning.

One is that law enforcement and criminal justice systematically ignore the more serious victimization of the poor—that by the rich. If an impetus for protecting poor victims is deemed an imperative for social justice (with the reasoning that the people who can least protect themselves should be protected), then concentration on punishing the poor through law is a greater perversion of the principle than no enforcement at all. Protecting the poor by punishing the poor may be a convenient rationalization, but it is morally indefensible.

The other hole is belief in the fallacy that punishment of offenders helps victims. Incarceration makes an offender no less dangerous upon release than immediate discharge. If an offender is dangerous enough to be imprisoned today, that offender cannot be projected to have become less dangerous when released. Insofar as communities are made safer by incarcerating offenders at all, they are made more dangerous by releasing them ever. Conviction, and to a lesser extent arrest, increase the likelihood that some offenders will resort to committing new crimes after they get out of jail, and hence put citizens at greater risk of victimization than ever.

Victims of most offenses are at minimal risk of a return visit from an offender. As police know, people such as abused wives who usually *do* risk repeated offenses are likely to suffer more rather than less by offenders who have been embittered by being jailed. Criminal courts seldom order compensation to victims, and even if they do, payment is problematic. Police rarely return stolen property. Victims are carefully separated from criminal defendants so that there are practically no chances for direct venting of grievances, and, as shown in many studies, abstract knowledge that an offender is being punished in some unwitnessed way offers little satisfaction. Victims who are called to testify often suffer the frustration of continued appearances and delays in trial proceedings and can be subject to humiliation on the witness stand. All in all, those who are fortunate enough to have losses insured will get far more satisfaction from these payments than they will from anything the criminal-justice system has to offer. Nor does the criminal-justice system reduce risk of victimization in the community as a whole. Insofar as poor victims pay taxes, criminal justice is probably more cost to them than benefit.

Poor victims deserve protection, to be sure. But it is farcical to justify punishing poor offenders on this pretext.

Should Criminal Justice Be Abolished?

If the activity of the police, the courts, and criminal corrections agencies is so immoral and ineffectual, it is tempting to conclude that criminal-justice agencies should be abolished. But in social processes, as in biological ones like embryo development, it is foolish to hold that processes gone wrong can be corrected by simple reversal. When police strike, disorder is likely to result. Abolition of criminal-justice agencies would provide the wrong signal to a people who have grown dependent on them. To prevent wide-spread public panic and the possibility that police, fearing for their jobs, would inflame emotions of the citizens or even riot themselves, de-emphasis of the importance of law enforcement has to be gradual.

Ironically, if criminal-justice officials could be made to feel more secure in their own livelihoods, they would ease off on law enforcement. It might be a good idea, therefore, to guarantee them life tenure, as we do federal judges, with the promise that their good salaries will keep pace with inflation. Moreover, society would be generally better served by a more seasoned and smaller personnel force, and to this end the criminal-justice system would do well to review existing retirement policies, with a view both toward extending terms of service and moving somewhat slower to replace retirees. There is a pronounced tendency among police—the gatekeepers of criminal justice—to mellow as they grow older. They become more relaxed about handling disputes and are more inclined to deal with problems informally, appreciating that taking people into custody or filing offense reports is often wasted effort. A lot can be said for letting criminal-justice forces relax and mature.

Meanwhile, the primary impetus for doing without law enforcement has to come from citizens. Insofar as they can control one another's behavior privately and can develop mechanisms for mediating disputes among themselves, they can lessen the force of criminal justice by benign neglect. Rather than fighting criminal justice, citizens would do better to learn to live without it.

Social Justice

As a substitute for law enforcement, informal mediation of disputes by the people concerned is capable of reducing inequalities between treatment of rich and poor.

Mediation means that someone trusted by antagonists encourages both sides to air their views and grievances, to listen to and empathize with the other's concerns, to suggest ways in which they might be able to meet each other's concerns, and to continue negotiations until both sides agree that the terms are satisfactory. In traditional China, mediation was concluded by a tea ceremony in which the grievants toasted one another and thanked the mediator. In our society, it would be more customary for grievants to conclude by signing a contract. Whatever the ceremony, it symbolizes that the parties have reconciled their differences and arranged a way in which they can continue to live together congenially.

In Indiana a group calling itself PACT (Program to Advance Community Treatment) is helping communities establish "VORPs" (Victim-Offender Reconciliation Programs). How VORP works can be seen in the case of a seventeen-year-old man who burglarized and ransacked the home of an older woman who lived alone. A VORP worker asked whether the victim would be willing to meet the offender. When she agreed, the offender was approached, and he also agreed. It is a moot point whether the victim or the offender was more apprehensive about the encounter. They met with the mediator in the victim's home. The victim first described her loss—both the dollar amount and sentimental attachment to goods stolen and damaged. She also described her fear at discovering the violation of her premises, and over the prospect that the predator might return and even attack her. In his turn, the youth reported that the stolen goods had been sold and could not be recovered. He assured the woman that the thought of returning to the scene of the crime had never entered his mind. Eventually, the mediator negotiated a restitution schedule which the youth could meet and which satisfied the victim, who by now was considerably relieved and even found the offender likeable. She also found that she no longer cared that much about monetary compensation. For his part, the offender showed considerable contrition and chagrin upon realizing how badly he had hurt the victim. The victim and offender signed a restitution agreement, and shook hands in parting.

It is clear that mediation will not always work and that victims should not be coerced into it. But a number of cases that now end up in the courts might be susceptible to this kind of handling. Obviously, the diversion of cases from the criminal-justice system would have to begin with the easier cases, the more serious ones being left to formal prosecution. In a society that keeps moving toward imprisonment for types of offenders who would previously have been left at liberty, a shift in emphasis the other way would represent real progress.

In societies where mediation is well established, it is common for mediators to be senior members of communities who are known and respected by both sides, and not bureaucrats. Instead of believing that a mediator needs to be disinterested in disputes to settle them fairly, as Americans would be inclined to do, both sides trust the mediator because the mediator has a strong personal stake in their leading happy, productive, and peaceful lives in the community. Whether we can develop communities in which such respected persons can emerge remains to be seen.

This kind of informal handling of disputes is less unjust than law enforcement in several ways. As criminologist Richard Korn has observed, mediation and restitution mechanisms are well established among persons of means in the United States, especially for the resolution of business disputes. If informal handling gradually displaced law enforcement, the poor would gain a privilege now largely reserved to the middle and upper classes.

Indications from victim surveys and from official records are that, in an overwhelming number of cases, victims of street crime come from the same economic class as the criminal. Even if victims or offenders gained unfair advantage in mediation settlements, poor victims would still generally get more than they now do from punishment of offenders, and poor offenders would be on equal footing instead of fighting against persons of wealth and position. If not eliminated, class discrimination in the handling of disputes would at least be reduced.

A characteristic of settlements negotiated face-to-face between disputants is that they tend to be less extreme than the sanctions imposed in criminal courts. Face-to-face contact and ongoing social ties constitute by far the strongest restraint on violence and predation that human beings have going for them. Taking offenders out of communities and punishing them according to law loosens those restraints.

In the final analysis, it must be acknowledged that perfect social justice is unimaginable, let alone unattainable. The settlement of disputes entails a shift in the balance of power between grievants. If we examine any mechanism for handling disputes closely enough, we can expect to find that some groups fare worse than others—perhaps women worse than men in disputes between them, or the young and the elderly worse than the middle-aged, or those with fewer years of schooling worse than others. The moral imperative for approaching social justice requires that we pursue the search for inequity in any mechanism, and experiment with ways to reduce the level of injustice we discover.

For now, the unequal treatment of rich and poor under the law is the grossest form of injustice in American society. Yet the scope of law enforcement is continuing to expand rapidly. We can certainly imagine and try to implement better, less unjust alternatives even if we do not expect them to be flawless themselves. While criminal justice cannot be made less unjust by putting more effort into it, our handling of disputes can lessen injustice if we turn away from law enforcement.

"Drug addition causes crime."

"The use of drugs has become more extensive and pervasive, and when you have people selling drugs, you have guns, rivalries, rip-offs, and inevitably, violence."

James Sullivan
Chief of Detectives
New York City Police Department
1983

TEENAGERS SIT huddled in a darkened school cafeteria watching a film in which the main character sticks a needle into a vein in his arm. It is difficult, however, to distinguish detail because the room he sits in is lit only by a candle that reflects off a spoon and a small plastic bag. The addict heats the white crystalline powder, with a little water, in a spoon over the flame. When the heroin is dissolved, he fills his syringe and presses the plunger. The camera zooms in on his thin unshaven face; it has sores all over it. He does not look well.

A voice from the screen says, "To be a drug addict is to be one of the walking dead. The teeth are rotted out, the appetite is lost, and the stomach and intestines don't function properly. The gall bladder becomes inflamed;

95

eyes and skin turn a bilious yellow; in some cases the nose turns a flaming red; breathing is difficult...Sex organs become affected." An addict in a straightjacket stretches across the screen. The voice continues, "Imaginary and fantastic fears blight the mind and sometimes complete insanity results. Often times, too, death comes—much too early in life. Such is the torment of being a drug addict; such is the plague of being one of the walking dead." Thus, early in their lives, are most Americans educated in the "evils" of heroin.

In reality, many heroin addicts look as healthy and act as normally as most people. They can have good builds and look quite fit. Far from the stereotype of the trembling junkie, addicts often go undetected in the business world, and number among the successes. Misconceptions about heroin addiction abound.

Demystification

Information on heroin is plentiful. Heroin is derived from opium. Morphine, the chief active ingredient of opium, is heated with acetic acid creating heroin, which is then converted back into morphine when it enters the body. When morphine reaches the brain, it is treated as if it were endorphins, a naturally occuring chemical in the body. Endorphins somehow (science does not know exactly) affect behavior and mood. Long-distance running, for example, produces endorphins which leads to a feeling of well being and creates an addiction. The runner who takes days off feels depressed. The chemical make-up of morphine and endorphins is exactly the same, so the brain treats morphine the same as endorphins.

The use of opiates (opium and its derivatives) has a long history in the United States and the world. We know opium use is at least as ancient as the Sumerians (7000 B.C.). They named the opium poppy "the plant of joy." In 1806 morphine was separated from the other components that make opium, and in 1874 the process by which morphine is converted to heroin was discovered. The main uses of opiates are medicinal, used for tranquilization, sedation, sleep, relief of coughing and diarrhea, and the relief of pain.

It is doubtful that opiates have harmful effects. A 1928 study published in the American Medical Association's (AMA) Archives of Internal Medicine found that "addiction is not characterized by physical deterioration or impairment of physical fitness aside from the addiction per se. There is no evidence of change in the circulatory, hepatic, renal or endocrine functions. When it is considered that these subjects had been addicted for at least five years, some of them for as long as twenty years, these negative observations are highly significant." A search of the literature conducted in 1956 by the Canadian province, British Columbia, disclosed no studies on the proved harmful effects of addiction among the more than five hundred reports surveyed. An article in the *Bulletin of the World Health Organization* concluded that "harm to the individual is, in the main, indirect, arising from preoccupation with drug-taking; personal neglect, malnutrition and infection are frequent consequences." Edward Brecher and the editors of *Consumer Reports* were unable to find even one study of the proved harmful effects of heroin for their excellent book, *Licit and Illicit Drugs*, published in 1972. The overwhelming conclusion that one reaches from reviewing studies of the physical health of addicts is that opiates result in no measurable organic damage.

If one can believe the research, there are also no evil psychological effects of opiate addiction. It does not cause mental impairment. A study conducted in part by the Assistant Surgeon General of the United States in 1938 found that of three thousand addicts not one suffered from a psychosis caused by opiates. A 1946 study compared six hundred addicts with six hundred non-addicts and reached the same conclusion. And, in 1963, Deputy Commissioner Henry Brill of the New York State Department of Mental Hygiene and chairman of the AMA's narcotic committee bluntly stated, "In spite of a very long tradition to the contrary, clinical experience and statistical studies clearly prove that psychosis is not one of the pains of addiction. Organic deterioration is regularly produced by alcohol in sufficient amounts but is unknown with opiates."

In truth, poor health among addicts must be attributed to the illegality of opiates. Many states require a prescription to obtain a hypodermic syringe, denying the addict access to the tools of addiction. Unfortunately, the addict must continue to take the drug. Needles are often in short supply and, therefore, are reused. Diseases spread rapidly as addicts share needles, especially since the needles are rarely sterilized.

In addition, addicts must worry about the contents of their purchases because drugs bought on the street are almost never pure. Substances added to the drug often cause illness and death.

The illegality of opiates also ensures that the street price of the drug will be high. The cost of an addiction can easily be between $20 and $100 a day, forcing addicts to devote a large share of their time and financial resources to obtaining their daily drug. Other items, such as food and medical care, come second.

The list of health problems associated with the criminalization of the addict is long. One cause of these problems seems particularly vile. Addicts known to the police are often arrested or brought in for questioning. The addict, deprived of opiates, soon begins withdrawal symptoms and, although withdrawal is rarely fatal, constant resubmission to withdrawal symptoms helps add to the addicts' health problems.

All opiates are addicting. That is, prolonged and daily use of any of the drugs creates a physical dependence. When not deprived of the drug, the addict shows no unusual behavior, and continued use in uniform amounts produces a tolerance to most of the effects. Lack of opiates, however, causes the addict to enter withdrawal— somewhat comparable to a horrible three-day case of either food poisoning, flu, or allergic reaction. All the addict desires is the drug he or she is being deprived of. Addicts hate withdrawal.

Neither physical nor mental addiction to heroin is cured by withdrawal. No study has demonstrated that more than 10 percent of those who can "kick the habit" stay off heroin. Most show far less. A California study examined 3,300 addicts committed to state facilities between 1961 and 1968. Only 300 were able to leave the programs, and it is questionable that even these 300 were no longer addicts. Another study is illustrative. In 1955, 247 addicts were admitted to Riverside Hospital in New York. Three years later, only eight were unaddicted, unhospitalized, unimprisoned, and alive. All eight, however, swore they had never been addicted, and patient records support this for seven of the eight. There has never been a rehabilitation program that could put opiate addicts back into the community unaddicted.

Early references to the use of opium indicate that addiction was not defined as a problem. No doubt, people were addicted to opium, but addicts do not behave or act noticeably different from their neighbors. Addiction only becomes noticeable when one enters withdrawal. Early opiate addicts merely consumed more opium whenever they began to feel ill. Possibly, such addicts never realized that the opium they consumed caused their illness and, at the same time, cured it.

Opiate use in this country in the early 1800s was minimal. Since the U.S. did not grow or tax opium it can be safely assumed that importation of opium was related to usage, and the evidence is that measurable opiate use in this country started about 1840. Consumption rose rapidly in the 1870s, a trend attributable to many factors, among them medical science, the Civil War, the patent medicine industry, and physicians.

Rise of Addiction Rates

Nineteenth-century scientists played a large role in the spread of opiate addiction. A major step was the isolation of morphine from opium in 1806. Morphine is easier to use than opium, which is not of a consistent potency. For this reason physicians regularly prescribed morphine, even though it is approximately ten times more powerful than opium.

With the introduction of the hypodermic syringe in 1853, the use of morphine spread rapidly. This scientific development allowed physicians to inject morphine directly into muscle, causing the drug to act more quickly. It was first used extensively during our Civil War when morphine was commonly given to relieve pain and alleviate dysentary. Many soldiers left the battle field addicted.

The patent medicine industry of the late 1800s greatly increased the number of addicts in the U.S. civilian population. These companies claimed to have products that would soothe almost any problem and, since regulation was lacking, ingredients contained in the product were not required to be listed on the package. In addition, manufacturers produced "cures" for addiction that contained opium or morphine. Patent medicines were available without prescriptions in drugstores, grocery stores, general stores, and by mail. Their names speak of another era: Ayer's Cherry Pectoral, Mrs. Winslow's Soothing Syrup, Darby's Carminative, Godfrey's Cordial, McMunn's Elixer of Opium, and Dover's Powder—to name but a few.*

Physicians in the 1800s did not enjoy the status they do today, in part because of their inability to cure disease. They practiced a brand of medicine that consisted largely of leeches and laxatives, which required the patient to have a strong constitution. Often, the patient would be killed by the cure. Opiates, in contrast, were mild and effective. A single shot of morphine would greatly decrease the patient's awareness of his symptoms, make him feel better generally, and, not insignificantly, happy that the doctor had helped. Opiates satisfied the physicians' need to have something that worked in a world where they knew nothing. According to a study conducted shortly after 1900, physicians were responsible for one half of the addicted population.

Studies of opiate users, circa 1800 in the Midwest, reveal that women addicts outnumbered their male counterparts by at least a six to four margin. By that time, opiates had proved to be an effective pain killer for menstrual and menopausal discomfort. In addition, a woman faced much less social disapproval drinking her

---

*The belief that one can get "high" by taking aspirin and Coca-Cola probably stems from this period. Coke, at the time, contained cocaine. Mixing one of the opiated pain killers, e.g. Godfrey's Cordial, with Coke would have created an effect far in excess of what either of the items would do separately.

medicine than drinking alcohol. Quite likely, the majority of addicts were professional males and their menopausal spouses.

At the turn of the century, an estimated 200 to 250 thousand Americans from all levels of society were addicted. It is noteworthy that then, as now, physicians were the most addicted population. An estimated 2 percent of physicians were addicts while other professional groups (lawyers and pharmacists, for example) had an estimated rate of .7 percent, compared to an estimated .2 percent for the general population.

In 1896, importation of opiates declined and, just as the rise in addiction in the late 1800s was due to many factors, its decrease following 1896 was also influenced from many sides. Among the factors that led to the decrease were public awareness of addiction and market saturation.

The general public was unaware of the addicting quality of opiates for most of the nineteenth century. Few public statements about addiction were made by either medical people or government officials. Physicians who knew that opiates were addicting might pass this information along to their patients, but most doctors lacked that knowledge. The patent medicine industry was disinclined to inform customers of the habit-forming effect of opiates because such information might lead people to discontinue use of the products and lead to lower sales. The industry strongly fought efforts that would have required disclosure on labels that their products contained opium. Thus, customers who knew that opiates were addicting might consume the drug unwittingly in unmarked medicines or under the impression that they were taking cures for addiction.

Public awareness of the addicting capacity of opiates was partly due to a general reform movement in the United States in the late 1800s. The public was angered and frightened by the ability of large companies to do as they saw fit; the ability of the patent medicine industry to market products that hid the fact that they contained opiates was a glaring example. Many writers of the period decried the situation and urged legislation to curb the abuses. The rising temperance movement helped. Most people opposed to alcohol use were also opposed to opiates.

Ironically, the introduction of heroin to consumers in 1898 was the result of growing concern with addiction. Thought to combat the withdrawal symptoms of morphine, heroin replaced morphine in many of the patent medicines. Bayer, which introduced it commercially, advertised "heroin for coughs."*

It is likely that the decrease in the use of opiates was due to market saturation as well. Following the growth of opiate use in 1870, there was a slow and steady increase until the mid 1890s. This pattern of consumption is similar to the pattern of growth one would expect for any popular consumer item whether it be hula hoops, bubble gum, or sliced bread. The product is introduced; consumer knowledge grows; people who want the product buy it; and soon most people who want the product have purchased it. Sales growth slows or stops completely.

The above factors produced an environment that was right for some type of legislation aimed at curbing the use of opiates. Addiction had been defined as a problem and reformists of the period believed that the government could change people's behavior by well-written laws and good enforcement.

---

*In truth, heroin acts more quickly and with greater intensity than morphine and is as addicting. The fact that Bayer and other companies saw fit to use the new "nonaddicting" substance is strong evidence that the public was quite aware of the problem of addiction and wished to avoid it.

Some states passed laws restricting or forbidding the use of opiates. They had little effect. A ban on the sale of opium in one state did not prevent its importation from another. Anti-opium groups therefore turned to the federal government. They pointed out that the United States had called for a world conference on opium to convene in 1909, and cited the absence of a national law on opium as a possible embarrassment to U.S. representatives at the meeting.

Three major commercial groups in our country greatly affected the first federal legislation: pharmacists, physicians, and the patent medicine industry. As David Musto describes in his book, *The American Disease,* pharmacists wished to see a ban on patent medicines containing opiates because a ban on narcotics in patent medicines would give pharmacists almost a total monopoly on the distribution of opiates. Physicians also wanted a ban on opiated patent medicines because they wanted the sole right to authorize the use of opiates. The patent medicine industry opposed the ban on opiates, realizing that the removal of narcotics from their medicines would spell the demise of the industry.

At first, it appeared that the deadlock between the two positions would mean that no federal legislation on opiates would be enacted. A ban on the importation of smoking opium was passed by Congress as a compromise before the world conference. Neither pharmacists, nor physicians, nor the patent medicine industry would be hurt by the law. The only group that smoked opium was the Chinese and they had little power in this country at that time. An official of the American Pharmaceutical Association, arguing for a ban on smoking opium, said, "If the Chinaman cannot get along without his 'dope,' we can get along without him."

The principal legislation in this country aimed at controlling the use of opiates is the Harrison Act of 1914. The intention of the law is to bring the distribution of opiates under tighter control. It requires a nominal tax, the use of special forms when transferring opiates, and a requirement that those who dispense the drugs be registered to do so. Its passage marked a major victory for medical doctors and a crushing defeat for patent medicines. The act only allowed small amounts of opiates in proprietary medicines—one quarter grain of heroin, for example, to each ounce. It permits the dispensing of stronger dosages only given by a physician, dentist, or veterinary surgeon for "legitimate medical purposes," and "prescribed in good faith." Health-care providers other than doctors were thereby effectively denied access to the major medical tool of this millenium.

In addition, addicts are denied easy access to opiates. It does not appear that the Harrison Act intended to deny opiates to addicts; neither addicts nor addiction are mentioned in the law. Early Supreme Court decisions, however, soon closed almost all legal avenues.

Supreme Court Decisions

In 1915 the United States Supreme Court ruled that possession of smuggled drugs was a crime. The decision meant that one could legally possess only opiates dispensed by a physician. By 1922 the high court had ruled that dispensing the drug to an addict "for the purpose of providing the user with morphine sufficient to keep him comfortable by maintaining his customary use" was not a legitimate medical purpose. Addiction was effectively criminalized.

Two major factors led the Supreme Court to the above decisions. First, there was a widespread belief that opiate addiction was curable. Many physicians opened clinics to cure addiction in the early 1900s and reported tremendous success in ending addictions. Some clinics were able to gain government support for the effectiveness of their treatments. It was not until the 1930s that officials realized that withdrawal of narcotics does not constitute a cure. Within about five to ten days the body will no longer exhibit the uncontrolled symptoms associated with withdrawal from opiates, but the addict soon starts using the drug again. As was noted earlier, no rehabilitation program has been succesful in putting addicts back on the streets without drugs. At the time of the Supreme Court decisions, however, this was not known. It appeared to the Court that those who continued their addictions did so because of personal vice. Addicts were thought to be sick individuals who chose to remain sick.

The second major factor that contributed to the Court's decisions is related to the belief that addiction is curable. The passage of the Harrison Act gave physicians a virtual monopoly on the distribution of opiates, which allowed some physicians to make large amounts of money prescribing them. The Court acted to end this promiscuous distribution of narcotics on the belief that such physicians were keeping people addicted. Once again, the Court believed that, if the opiates were withdrawn from the patients' use, the addiction would be cured.

The Crime Cost

The cost of an addiction often requires the addict to steal or turn to prostitution, and the losses due to crimes committed by addicts are believed to be high. It is estimated, for example, that one-half of the burglaries and robberies in New York City are the work of addicts. The money that the addict takes from the public to pay for drugs often goes into the coffers of large crime organizations which allow them to expand into legitimate businesses where they continue to employ their criminal tactics.

Furthermore, we spend millions of dollars on law enforcement in a vain effort to end the illicit importation of opiates. The entire addict population of the U.S. consumes less than five tons of heroin annually; very few successful heroin shipments are necessary before the demand is met. Enforcement activities only assure the successful importer high profits by cutting out competition. Heroin costing thousands of dollars in Europe or Asia eventually sells for millions on the streets of the U.S. With the possibility of such huge profits, there will always be some one willing to undertake the business of supplying addicts with narcotics. In addition, the successful confiscation of heroin does not guarantee that it will never reach the streets. The movie, *The French Connection*, was based on a true story. The heroin that was seized in that case later disappeared from the police evidence room, most likely ending up on the streets of New York.

Conclusions

This chapter has concentrated on opiate addiction, admittedly one of the less dangerous forms of drug addiction (alcohol use probably being the worst). The arguments for the legalization of addiction, however, are valid for the other drugs as well. Nicotine and amphetamines are harmful to the mind and body of a user and to society, but the criminalization of the addict does more harm than good. An addict is not helped by prison, and society is not helped by spending the amount of money needed to keep him there.

Still, maintenance of an opiate addiction should be legalized, even if we are not ready to legalize all drugs. Addicts certified by a physician should be allowed to obtain a daily amount of narcotic sufficient to prevent the onset of withdrawal. England, for example, uses a system of clinics where certified addicts are able to purchase their daily dose. The addict can easily and safely obtain the drug at an affordable price and thus has no need to turn to crime or suffer poor health to support a habit. The addict and society both benefit from such an arrangement.

The ability of an addict to obtain legally his or her drug will not suddenly end all the evils that have occurred because of the criminalization of addiction. Many individuals who steal will continue to steal. They will probably steal less, however.

A number of positive outcomes should occur from legalization. Addicts' health would improve. Most of the profit for illegal traffickers would end. The resultant decrease in pushers might reduce the number of addicts. New addicts would no longer represent a future source of income for the pusher. And finally, we would save billions of dollars on law enforcement. No longer would we pay other countries to cut their opium production. No longer would we employ people to prevent opiate smuggling. No longer would we house thousands of addicts in our prisons and jails. No longer would we treat the addict as an animal undeserving of human compassion.

"Community corrections is a viable alternative."

Undoubtedly, many offenders—especially those whose problems are more social than criminal—can be screened out of the correctional system without danger to the community, especially a community where remedies for their problems can be obtained through existing noncorrectional resources. The juvenile court intake and referral methods have proved the value of this policy of diversion. Application of a similar system to adult cases could reduce court dockets and correctional caseloads. Criteria for the diversion of adult offenders from the correctional process need to be developed, and, to support the policy and practice of diversion, community agencies must cooperate by extending their services to offenders.

National Council on Crime and Delinquency, 1967

IN THE MID-NINETEENTH CENTURY penologists were first struck that people were being put in prison who did not belong there, and who were made worse for the experience. The first American response: to put young, less serious offenders in "reformatories" where they would not have to mingle with hardened criminals, and where inmates would have greater chance for rehabilitation.

By the 1880s, overcrowded reformatories were declared to be failures. There was no sign that they were rehabilitating offenders, and prisons had more inmates than ever. One might have supposed that reformatories would be closed down, but no. In light of the perceived increasing danger posed by crime, they now became regarded as necessary evils, another part of the prison system providing space for the expanding supply of inmates. Many young offenders who would previously have been set free were now put in jail.

British criminologist Stanley Cohen has termed this phenomenon "widening the net," and it has been recurring regularly for the past hundred years. It would be one thing if reformers had intended to widen the net; what they in fact intended was to channel people from incarceration to more benign supervision.

Highlights of Diversionary Reform

Three major reforms were introduced at the close of the nineteenth century. One was probation. Here, convicts are sentenced to a term of community supervision under employees of the courts, remaining free on condition of good behavior. Judges have imposed such requirements of good behavior as refraining from drink, avoiding contact with known felons, holding particular jobs, keeping appointments with probation officers, and traveling from the county or marrying only with the probation officer's permission and, of course, not committing offenses. If any of the conditions of probation are violated, the probation officer is entitled to petition the court to revoke probation and send the offender to jail or prison, either for a term that had previously been set and suspended, or for any term permitted by law. Defendants have few procedural rights in revocation hearings. The United States Supreme Court, for instance, has refused to rule that probationers who face imposition of a suspended sentence have a right to be represented by counsel.

A corollary reform is parole. Parole boards, who typically were appointed by state governors (or for the federal system, by the president), were once given wide latitude to release prison inmates before expiration of their sentence. Conditions of parole paralleled those for probation, and parole officers could petition the boards for revocation, requiring the offender to serve the remainder of his term. In recent years, many jurisdictions have sought to restrict the powers of parole boards. In 1977 the Indiana parole board lost the prerogative of releasing inmates early. Inmates there typically earn one day's good time for each day of the sentence served and then are paroled for the remainder of the sentence, subject again to revocation.

The third reform was the juvenile court. Defendants too young to be tried as adults have closed hearings before juvenile referees or judges, who decide not whether the public deserves to have the defendant punished, but what treatment is in the best interests of the child. The idea that the court should act as benevolent guardian of children's interests is known as the *parens patriae* doctrine. The court is not restricted to hearing allegations that children have committed criminal offenses, but also considers allegations of "status offenses," such as truancy, running away from home, generally being incorrigible, or even allegations of parental neglect. Any of these circumstances can cause the court to commit juveniles to confinement in training schools until parole authorities there deem them ready for release, or until they turn twenty-one. In 1967, in the case entitled *In Re Gault*, a majority of the United States Supreme Court decided that *parens patriae* was empty rhetoric, that juveniles were subject to even greater confinement than they would be if tried as adults, and that defendants in juvenile court were entitled to most due process rights given adult defendants, such as right to counsel and right to confront witnesses. (The Supreme Court later refused to require that juveniles be given jury trials, reverting to rhetoric about the distinct nature of juvenile hearings.)

These reforms were designed to divert offenders from prison and, according to historian David Rothman, at first they worked. But in the 1920s, disenchantment prevailed, the belief spreading that coddling criminals did not rehabilitate them and that they needed good doses of old-fashioned punishment. Prison populations rose to record levels, with the diversion programs raising the number of people in criminal-justice custody to previously unimaginable levels. Today, prisons are bigger and more tightly packed than ever; at a rough guess (available figures are outdated or incomplete), about 150,000 juveniles are confined, several hundred thousand offenders are on parole, and 1.5 million are on probation (compared to over 400,000 inmates in prisons, and more than 200,000 in jails). Diversion, indeed!

The halfway house was introduced in Britain in the 1950s and in the United States with a raft of other programs a decade later. It was thought that offenders could be more easily rehabilitated if they were confined in the community instead of prisons—and at much less expense.

The President's Commission on Law Enforcement and Administration of Justice heartily endorsed community corrections in 1967. Shortly thereafter, the U.S. Department of Labor began funding pilot versions of a new level of diversion—pretrial diversion—in which defendants with little or no prior record who agreed to plead guilty as charged and either to take jobs or to go to school received provisional convictions. After ninety days or six months of good behavior, the charges against the defendant would be dropped. California went so far as to pay counties what were called "probation subsidies" for reducing numbers of inmates they committed to the state prison system.

Incarceration fell off substantially between 1960 and 1975; but by the mid-1970s, a backlash set in. In California, for example, the parole board began subverting probation subsidies by requiring inmates to serve more of their terms, causing prisons to fill again. In some programs, like California's Youth Treatment Project, those who worked with offenders temporarily managed to reduce recidivism by acting as political sponsors for their clients, helping offenders become legitimately established in the community. However, as criminologist William Selke found in a study of other youth centers, workers in the program soon lost the spirit of working as sponsors, and began talking, thinking, and acting just like correctional supervisors of old. Disenchantment with community diversion programs grew from within and without. The belief that offenders needed punishment and tight discipline regained currency. Community-corrections programs did not die but were given more and more clients who otherwise would have been set free by the courts without restrictions. Prisons, jails, and juvenile institutions have again filled to record levels.

It has been interesting for the present authors to follow recent developments in their own community, Bloomington, Monroe County, Indiana. The State Department of Correction has wanted to open a work release center in Bloomington, but has been frustrated so far by residents' objections to having offenders living in their midst. Were the center to open, most of the space would be reserved for state prisoners to serve out the last half-year of their sentences, but about twenty-five beds would be available for use by local judges as a sentencing alternative. Some of the judges have expressed the desire to have the space to send defendants they now feel impelled to release into the community on ordinary probation. An array of other programs are in use, such as requiring offenders to do public service work, or sentencing them to "house arrest," under which they can leave their homes only for necessities. At the same time, commitments to state prison remain at least steady, and the jail is being used to give more offenders than ever a taste of punishment. Only a few community activists question whether incarceration should be so much used. Practically without exception, local officials fall into two groups: those who say that the level of incarceration is just about right, and those who say that more jail and prison space is needed. It is those in the latter category who are more inclined to look favorably on further development of community programs. Here the reality of diversion programs is laid bare: regardless of the good intentions of reformers who conceive them, they become dominated by the official inclination to do more to offenders rather than less. From the reformatory to the halfway house, programs introduced to divert offenders from incarceration have proved to be a pretext, or sometimes a mere facade for extending confinement.

Why Diversion Fails

There is one country that in recent years has seemed to divert successfully. In Sweden, the incarceration rate has fallen substantially and other than one secure old-style prison in Stockholm, the prisons that survive confine less rigorously. Offenders in these institutions are generally free to leave for the day to work outside, and are scarcely locked in even at night. Prisoners are unionized, and livable and humane prison conditions have become a matter of right.

The Swedes proceed on the premise that much of a person's strength and capacity to contribute to others comes from social support. State welfare support is seen not as charity, but as the very foundation of a productive social order, and care and support are seen not as a privilege granted by an altruistic state, but as a matter of basic human rights the state exists to serve. If people are sick or wayward, the state owes them whatever treatment and support it takes for them to become well established in the social mainstream. Swedes have far fewer problems than Americans in believing that offenders whose needs are greater than those of ordinary citizens have a claim to a disproportionate share of tax-generated resources. If a prisoner's union can help articulate what kind of support is truly helpful to offenders, then the union has a vital role to play in helping the Swedish state achieve crime control. And the system seems to work, for on the whole, recidivism among Swedish offenders is remarkably low. To the Swedes, diverting offenders from prison, like diverting parents from jobs to care for infants, is simply good business practice, which gives a good return on their taxes.

Americans tend to believe that those who have most to contribute to society need no state assistance. Money the socially able pay in taxes is seen as inhibiting their ability to invest in private enterprise, which in the majority view is the way the well-to-do can be most socially productive. As a corollary, Americans generally presume that there is something seriously wrong with a person who requires state assistance or treatment. In the current wave of unemployment, union leaders report that members who have been laid off are often reluctant to apply for unemployment benefits because doing so is seen as a sign of personal weakness.

The typical offender does not come into court asking for state assistance, but wants most to be left alone like any other self-respecting citizen. By committing crime, though, the offender has forced other Americans to pay tax dollars to protect themselves against further predation. The criminal is not asking nicely and humbly for welfare charity but is holding up the public for state assistance, and he is profoundly resented. So, when Americans pay for treatment of offenders, they do so in anger at what the offenders are forcing from them. If the welfare mother is an object of social scorn, the offender is an object of loathing. When treatment is given to offenders, citizens want it to hurt. And, if after they have been given treatment they are ungrateful enough to get back into trouble with the law, they should be hurt more. God forbid that prisoners should become unionized and make further demands on the public purse.

For some time, it has been the rule that offenders do not get sentenced to incarceration until they have accumulated substantial prior records. By that time, they are unlikely to be deemed worthy of diversion. The politics of the situation commonly requires that offenders have no prior record, or perhaps a single prior conviction, to qualify for a new community program. Workers in the program quickly lose the pioneer spirit, finding more established officials regard their clients with suspicion and contempt and that they must denigrate their clients to earn official respect. In addition, clients who feel inherently degraded by having treatment forced upon them are unlikely to demonstrate appreciation for the workers' efforts. Evaluation has begun to indicate that clients of new programs, such as those designed to have offenders pay restitution, are more likely to get into subsequent trouble with the law not because they commit new crimes, but because they fail to meet program requirements. Offenders are seen as less worthy because they have had a special break and failed to warm to it. The net effect is to reinforce the public perception that offenders ought to suffer more at the hands of criminal justice. The public pays more to have offenders pay more for their transgressions, and official attitudes harden further.

Not only do American values limit offenders' chances of being diverted, they also limit job opportunities for state employees. Given the scarcity of employment in the United States, state employees have special reason to try to hang onto their positions and prove the need for their services. In Sweden, officials can enhance their positions by demonstrating that their clients are satisfied with the services they receive. Client satisfaction helps demonstrate that state welfare for all citizens contributes to the strength of society and provides more evidence of what is to be gained from employing competent officials. By contrast, if clients of American state welfare and correction are satisfied with the services they receive, it is taken as a sign that something is wrong: wrong with the clients who are becoming more dependent on state services rather than learning self-reliance, and wrong with services that reward clients for being less socially deserving than independent citizens. Officials can hang onto their budgets only by demonstrating that clients are deteriorating and in need of their services. American values practically require that those who dedicate themselves to diverting offenders in fact widen the net of criminal confinement.

In theory there are two requirements for making diversion programs work. One is that officials of the programs act as political sponsors for their clients, in effect making communities safe for offenders. The other is that officials who decide whether to incarcerate agree to have their decisions monitored and to be guided toward using diversion only for defendants who otherwise would have been put in jail, prison, or a juvenile institution.

The first requirement could be met by a combination of changes. Correctional workers would have to be well connected to community people with power and status, such as major employers. They would also need autonomy from other criminal-justice officials. Probation officers, for instance, should not be subject to hiring and firing by a judge (as most are now) and, like lawyers, they would need to have privileged relations with their clients. The workers could impose no restrictions on clients, would have no power to revoke their probations or paroles—that would be left to police and prosecutors—and would be evaluated on their capacity to keep clients out of trouble with the law.

Miracles cannot be expected from political sponsorship, but it can be expected to reduce odds of recidivism among offenders with minimal prior records. Those with no prior records do best when left alone; and those with lengthy prior records remain poor risks no matter what is done to or for them. Traditional community supervision has at best no net impact on offenders, and at worst increases the danger that offenders pose to communities.

Criminologists have the tools to monitor official decisions to see whether they are in fact diversionary, and whether defendants referred to the program were those who previously would have been locked away. The catch is that officials and legislators involved have to have the political will to achieve diversion. Judges and prosecutors answer directly to electorates; other officials and correctional workers do so indirectly. An electorate that will tolerate diversion has to see state action in a new light—as something that promotes the general welfare by giving greater power to the clients of state services. Swedish experience suggests that this perspective rests on the more general view that practically all citizens require substantial state assistance to achieve full potential. Social control, if used, has to be presumed to be a constructive rather than restrictive exercise of power; it has to be seen primarily as the art of diversifying human activity and potential rather than as a mechanism for channeling and regulating human behavior.

This is not to say that Swedish ideas and practices can be directly imported into the United States; Sweden is a much smaller and more homogeneous country. For the time being at least, Swedes are more capable of establishing social peace by centralizing and unifying production and living conditions than Americans. Considerable experimentation and variation in forms of state support is appropriate to the American scene. The services that help Californians may well hinder Rhode Islanders. But the basic idea that government exists primarily to invest in the welfare of its citizens commends itself as much to Americans as it has to the Swedes.

Diversion, then, cannot be expected to occur in isolation. Americans need to believe that diversification rather than law makes people behave well. Popular will must support a broad range of state initiatives that enable citizens to establish cross-cutting networks of small enterprises—to build a new political economy over the ruins of capital-intensive, centralized production of goods and services. The treatment of offenders is just one more among many of our failing heavy industries. If we can begin the political change required to build a new economy, we can expect diversion of offenders to be a part of the package. Meanwhile, as matters stand, community corrections offers no alternative to the punishment of offenders, but merely extends the scope and scale of the punishment.

"The punishment can fit the crime."

The class was a graduate seminar in "Philosophical Issues of Law and Social Control." The teacher had just finished the introductory lecture, filling three blackboards with a proof in symbolic logic that there is no adequate justification for punishment.

A student asked, "What would you do if a man raped your daughter?"

"I'd try to reason with him."

"What if you couldn't reason with him?"

"I'd kill the sonuvabitch."

State University of New York at Albany, 1976

YOU MAY RECALL how Shylock lost his case in Shakespeare's *Merchant of Venice*. He had contracted to receive a pound of flesh if a borrower defaulted on a loan, and the court ruled in favor of Shylock's claim to the flesh after the borrower's default. Portia ordered a final judgment: yes, Shylock was entitled to his pound of flesh, but no more. If he cut out the slightest fraction more than a pound, or if so much as a single drop of blood fell out of the wound, Shylock would be in breach of the agreement and hence criminally liable for harm done. The court agreed, and Shylock was forced to abandon his quest for justice in favor of mercy.

During the past decade, many in the American-criminological community have been driven to Shylock's position. On one hand, they accept as fact that taking pounds of flesh from offenders neither rehabilitates them nor reduces crime. On the other hand, they figure a social contract has to be upheld, and that anyone who breaches the contract by breaking the law must be made to suffer in due measure by a just society. Lawyer/criminologist Andrew Von Hirsch has coined the term "just deserts" to refer to this ultimate rationale for punishment of offenders. The punishment should fit the crime—no more, no less.

The classical notion of retribution is known as *lex talionis*, or "an eye for an eye." If I blind someone in one eye and am blinded in turn, that is justice. But the equation will not precisely fit. If, for instance, I blind my victim without warning, then the victim suffers after the event, but not before. If I am then sentenced to be blinded in return, I suffer anticipation of the event as well. It is like taking a drop of blood along with the pound of flesh. Harm under one set of circumstances is bound to include elements that harm under other circumstances lacks. One reason some theologians postulate that vengeance must be left in God's hands and not given over to mere mortals is that, in the final analysis, we are incapable of constructing an equation that takes all circumstances and types of harm into account.

Punishment for crime is generally far less straightforward even than taking an eye for an eye. The most common form of punishment we use today is length of incarceration, but few of our prisoners are punished for confining others. Most are there for taking others' property without the owners' permission. French historian Michel Foucault has pointed out what a remarkable achievement it has been for Americans to decide that harm can be measured in days, months, and years. The human obsession for rationality drives people to think lives are interchangeable with machine parts whose cost and productive value can be quantified. So now the cost of a burglary can be measured against the length of time we deny a person's freedom. But when clearly thought about "How many years of a person's liberty equals the value of a lost television set?" has to be seen as an absurd question. The same applies to laying offenses along a scale of punishment. If you send your daughter to her room for 10 minutes for breaking a fifty-cent tumbler in a fit of anger, would you send her to her room for 13 days, 21 hours, and 20 minutes to uphold moral principle and teach her a lesson if she broke a $1,000 antique vase? You might well show your anger and demand that she help mend the vase as well as possible, but that bid for accountability and responsibility would scarcely be retributive—would hardly be punitive at all.

British criminologist Leslie Wilkins has carried the problem a step further by noting that crimes are not punished; offenders are. Attribution theorists like psychologist Joanne Joseph Moore have been studying how people assess the culpability of defendants. They find, for example, that jurors weigh a number of characteristics of victims and offenders. In the theft of a television, it would matter whether the jurors thought that the victim was an unattractive character who might have angered the offender, or whether the offender was thought to be a basically respectable person who came under an accomplice's evil influence, or whether the defendant seemed to smile rather than show remorse when the victim testified. Our criminal law recognizes some of this complexity, beginning with the requirement for most offenses not only that the defendant be found to have committed a wrongful act, but be found to have intended it. The law also allows other grounds for finding defendants not guilty, or for aggravating or mitigating offenses. Going further, sociologists Victoria Swigert and Ronald Farrell find that defendants charged with criminal homicide in an Eastern city were most likely to be convicted of first-degree murder rather than of lesser offenses if their physical appearance corresponded to the local psychiatric category, "normal primitive." Try as they might, human beings seem to be incapable of judging people by judging their acts alone, and their predispositions affect their decisions of how much harm a defendant has done and how long they should suffer for it.

Twenty years ago, sociologists Thorsten Sellin and Marvin Wolfgang put together a scale of seriousness of offenses from rankings that judges, police, and students gave to a set of crimes. Other researchers have since found that different categories of people produce much the same scale, both in the United States and in Canada. The problem is that real criminal cases entail real defendants and real complainants, so that in practice, those who assess offenses have room to feel considerable justification for concluding that one theft of $100 worth of property from a dwelling is more serious than another. Had Shylock been a surgeon trying to excise a one-pound tumor from a patient who objected on religious grounds, Portia might even have argued Shylock's case.

It is one thing to say that offenders ought to be given their just deserts. It is quite another to figure out what "just deserts" are.

Guidelines used by sentencing judges in various jurisdictions take several variables into account, including legal seriousness of offense charged, prior record, employment status, and bail status of the defendant. These guidelines have been found to predict whether defendants will be sent to jail with about 80 percent accuracy. It is harder to predict how long a jail sentence will be imposed, or what form or length of community supervision will be given. Meanwhile, experienced defendants report bewilderment over getting off when they have done something serious, and being severely sentenced when their guilt is questionable or their offense trivial. Cases are legion of co-defendants receiving widely disparate sentences.

A common exercise among those who teach criminal-justice courses is to give students hypothetical cases and ask them to decide which sentence should be imposed. The sentences asked for not only vary widely among students both for each case and across cases, but many times exceed the limits the law allows.

Consensus about punishment offenders deserve is limited in our society. This is not too surprising. The variety of offenses covered by penal codes is staggering; and the variety of circumstances of defendants' cases are greater still. Consensus would require that crime witnesses react with equal horror. It would require that witnesses readily cooperate in giving full information. More to the point, it would require substantial acknowledgment from about two million Americans currently serving sentences behind bars or in the community that they got their due, and all these views would have to coincide with penalties provided by law if the state were to embody retributive justice.

The problem goes further. Since, as we have seen, crime is so common among Americans, there is often dissensus as to whether punishment is deserved at all. For example, it is well documented that most middle-aged

Americans have at least experimented with marijuana, and that a substantial number of otherwise respectable Americans use it regularly. Possession of small amounts of the drug is completely legal only in Alaska, finable in some states, and remains a major felony punishable by years in prison in others. Cultivation of the plant for sale is a crime in all American jurisdictions, and yet a large and growing number of farmers—who would never use the drug themselves—have turned to cultivating this profitable cash crop. Some honest, hard-working growers are quite upset about criminals who try to steal from them, although of course they are in no position to ask for police protection or to take out insurance. Some people think those who are involved in the sale and distribution of marijuana ought to be lined up against a wall and shot. How on earth is consensus to be achieved?

A number of writers propose that so-called crimes without victims, like those involving marijuana, ought to be decriminalized or even legalized. That in itself, however, would not solve the problem for other crimes. How many people can candidly say they, or their nearest-and-dearest, never stole (perhaps equipment or food from work) or vandalized (perhaps kicked a vending machine or "toilet papered" a house), or assaulted (perhaps got in a minor scuffle) or trespassed, or lied for personal gain? These are the kinds of offenses that dominate criminal court dockets. How severely would we punish ourselves for our own crimes?

Consensus on punishment requires that criminals be truly extraordinary. They must do that which people generally find intolerable, practically unimaginable. We have little trouble agreeing that the crimes of John Wayne Gacy, or Steven Judy, or Charles Manson are outrageous, and although we may differ over the death penalty, we agree that their transgressions call for an extreme sanction. There is a consensus that burying young men in one's garden, or raping and strangling a strange woman and her children, or hanging and stabbing a pregnant woman in a ritual, is beyond our wildest fantasies. If a major city were to reserve punishment for something like the worst offender of the month, popular consensus might be achieved that a punishment constituted just deserts.

Controlling Punishment

To fit the crime, punishment not only needs to have a certain level, but needs to be swift and sure. If punishment is long delayed, the connection between it and the offense becomes strained. Retribution is an expression of moral outrage, of the passion of the moment over wrong done. It makes little sense to punish someone who has long been behaving properly for a transgression long past. That is the reason that statutes of limitation cut off prosecution for all but the most serious crimes after some time has elapsed.

Criminal-justice officials cannot help but be guided by conscience, and are inclined to believe in the justice of what they have done. If suddenly called upon to punish offenders more severely, they will do so more selectively and with greater deliberation. If called upon to punish more often, they will temper their severity. If called upon to speed up punishment, they will show more leniency and discharge more suspects or punish without taking evidence of innocence into account.

These patterns are well documented. In the eighteenth century, for example, the British Parliament made a number of offenses punishable by death. As the courts faced imposing death sentences in more kinds of crimes, informal settlement of cases rose to prominence, and most of those sentenced to death were reprieved. In the early 1970s, Governor Nelson Rockefeller sponsored legislation in New York State that mandated life sentences for those selling illicit drugs. Under the law, charges could not be reduced once defendants had been indicted. So police were less inclined to charge suspects with sale of drugs, prosecutors were more likely to charge defendants with a lesser offense like simple possession of drugs, defendants had little incentive to refrain from requesting jury trials which added to the judicial backlog, and conviction rates among those going to trial dropped as juries proved reluctant to convict on such serious charges. On the other hand, when penalties have been substantially reduced, as in Nebraska for possession of marijuana in the early 1970s, arrests and convictions have surged before settling down at a new plateau.

Since the 1950s, the Dutch have concentrated on increasing the likelihood that defendants brought to trial would get convicted. Convictions have increased, but in the process, delays in getting to trial are at the point at which many defendants seem to drop out of the system, and the severity of sentence has dropped to the point where it can be measured in days rather than months or years. The average daily population has remained roughly constant, at about 20 or 22 per 100,000 Dutch, the lowest known rate in the world.

In a study of experimental programs to reduce trial delay, political scientist Mary Lee Luskin found that punishment decreased by six days for every ten days' shortening of the time between the initial charging and the final court disposition. And as those who have been to traffic court—where "justice" is swift—can attest, penalties are not only light, but pleas of innocence are likely to be ignored in the rush of business: the innocent are nearly as subject to punishment as the guilty.

127

Suppose we want to make punishment both swift and sure, while closely controlling its severity. The problem of making these three elements of punishment coincide is similar to trying to hold the south poles of three electromagnets together. If you increase the electrical energy going through any of the magnets, it will tend to push the other magnets away. If you clamp down hard, you may be able to hold the magnets together awhile, but as your hand tires, they are likely to slip. In criminal justice, increasing the energy and attention devoted to any of the three elements of punishment will make the other two slip out of control.

As the current is turned down toward zero, holding the magnets together becomes relatively effortless. Similarly, a small criminal-justice force with practically no crime to respond to will be in a good position to respond swiftly, surely, and with measured severity to crimes that it handles. They will be able to devote singular attention to each offense. As rare and peculiar events, offenses will meet popular consensus that they are intolerable. Hence, citizens will more readily collaborate with law enforcement forces to put evidence together and to identify offenders. When the offender is brought to trial, the likelihood of conviction will be high, and consensus will be forthcoming on the punishment the clear and distinctive deviant deserves.

If criminal-justice officials are to make punishment swiftly and surely fit crimes, criminal justice must be a small and largely superfluous force in a practically crime-free society. If more resources are put into the criminal-justice system of a society with a high crime rate, the system will further break down and fail even more dismally to provide a just response to crime. This is exactly what has happened in the United States. As we have added personnel and money to an already large criminal-justice force, we have been confronted with a system that fills prisons with too severely punished minor offenders, manifestly fails to respond to most offenses, prolongs trial and punishment in cluttered courts, and is capricious about whom is punished and for how long.

Implications for Crime Control

Some advocates of retribution do not care whether punishment prevents crime. They argue that a citizenry deserves to have offenders punished regardless of whether punishment offers more than the satisfaction of moral indignation. If current attempts to build up law enforcement are only made to satisfy moral indignation, they are unjustified. Public dissatisfaction with delays, uncertainty, and improper severity will more than offset the desire for revenge.

Retribution can be thought to prevent crime, however. The state that shows itself capable of making punishments fit crimes can be assumed to earn public respect for its authority, and by extension, to earn public respect for its laws. A people who respect the state and its law can be expected to behave lawfully.

From another perspective, swift, sure punishment of controlled severity can be expected to deter people—both from committing a first offense and from committing additional crimes. It is important to recognize a key distinction between punishing for retribution and punishing for deterrence. For retribution, punishment is to be proportional to harm done by offenders; for deterrence, punishment is to cost offenders just more than they gain by committing offenses. At extremes, offenders who killed simply to take ten cents from their victims might be executed for the sake of retribution, and fined eleven cents to achieve deterrence. As Italian nobleman Cesare Beccaria wrote in the eighteenth century, a system designed to deter crime will generally impose far less severe punishments than one designed to achieve retribution. Since heavier punishments delay and reduce certainty of punishment, they impair its power to deter.

Still, consensus on light punishment is no easier to achieve with a massive criminal-justice system; and, a system that deters through punishment should have hardly any crime left to punish. From the perspective of deterrence, it is a sign of failure that a system that already punishes plentifully should be called upon to punish still more in order to prevent crime.

If anything, American criminal justice seems to play a role in promoting disrespect for law and order. Various independent estimates reach a common conclusion: Imprisoning growing numbers of offenders has at best a marginal effect on crime rates, since so many people fill the void by starting lives of crime. It may be that repressive criminal-justice systems here and elsewhere (as in Argentina, Chile, the Soviet Union, and South Africa) reflect or cause popular brutality. The fact remains that societies in which punishment is extensive have large and intractable problems of crime and violence. Societies that generate punishment generate crime, while relatively peaceful societies (the Netherlands and Japan, for example) find less pressure to punish.

There are more fundamental forces than criminal justice that enable people to live together peacefully. If we can slow down people's response to disputes so that they have time to act with greater deliberation and accommodation to needs of offenders and victims alike, there will be more of a chance that the punishment will fit the crime.

MYTH TEN

"Law makes people behave."

A punishment is an evil inflicted by public authority on him who hath done or omitted that which is judged by the same authority to be a transgression of the law, to the end that the will of men may thereby the better be disposed to obedience.... Before the institution of Commonwealth, every man had a right to everything, and to do whatsoever he thought necessary to his own preservation—subduing, hurting, or killing any man in order thereunto. And this is the foundation of that right of punishing, which is exercised in every commonwealth. For the subjects did not give the sovereign that right, but only in laying down theirs, strengthened him to use his own, as he should think fit, for the preservation of them all; so that it was not given, but left to him, and to him only, and (excepting the limits set him by natural law) as entire, as in the condition of mere nature, and of war of every one against his neighbor.

Thomas Hobbes, 1651

PROMINENT AS CRIME and punishment are in the media, Americans have come to equate law with social order. People are inclined to agree with English social philosopher Thomas Hobbes, that unless a strong sov-

131

ereign uses law enforcement to beat the citizenry into line, people will carry out a war of all against all among themselves. And yet it has been shown that law enforcement systematically ignores the major portion of crime, and has little effect on the rest. Some believe that this breakdown of law and order is a recent development, that it is because law enforcement is disintegrating that disorder is rising. There is no indication, however, that law enforcement was less selective or more effectual in the past, or that Americans endanger one another's life, liberty, or property today any more than a hundred years ago.

The State as a Source of Violence

In one respect, Americans have been relatively lucky. Although they employ a remarkably large criminal-justice force, they generally have not allowed one political faction to overpower another. Hence, the kind of violence that has recently resulted in the killing of thousands of Mayan Indians by Guatemalan government forces has been avoided. The one major exception is the five-year period of the Civil War where one in six American men was killed or wounded in combat, a statistic that horribly overshadows today's police homicide reports.

By creating monopolies on force, states have the greatest capacity to do harm to people, and they do so when officials become too bent on enforcing order. The mass slaughter of Jews by Nazis in Germany represents another example of how deadly people can become in the use of state apparatus. And of course, war among states poses the greatest threat to peace and order of all, to the very existence of humanity.

It is obvious that some kind of control is necessary to

restrain people from killing, raping, and pillaging one another. But it does not follow that the might of law enforcement creates this order by sending uniformed (or even plainclothes) forces to suppress the citizens.

Conditions Favoring Peace

Anthropologists have made an interesting discovery. Communities are more peaceful when ties of kinship cut across political lines. The prototype of the peaceful community is one that is matrilocal and patriarchal, that is, where men in political coalitions rule the communities, and where men move into the area occupied by their wives' families when they marry. If male political rivals start to fight in the community, it is likely that other men, who share blood ties with both disputants through marriage, will intervene to cut the fighting short. There has been a similar finding in London where family violence was lower in communities in which women stayed home and developed tight social networks with other wives. Husbands who had to answer to one another through concerted complaints from communities of wives were more restrained in their treatment of their own wives.

This does not imply that to keep the public peace women have to stay at home while men circulate. As a matter of social justice, women ought to be free to enjoy the same liberties as men. Happily, there are a number of other ways that cross-cutting ties can be established in communities.

Twenty years ago, urban planner Jane Jacobs described such communities in a much talked about book, *The Death and Life of Great American Cities*. She describes what she calls healthy urban neighborhoods as pockets in inner cities that may seem chaotic on the surface, but to the people who live, work, shop, eat, and drink there, are not only lively but safe and secure. She contrasts these neighborhoods to others that have deteriorated into filth, depression, and danger. Healthy neighborhoods are distinguished by their variety. Many activities take place there among high and low income people, old buildings are mixed with new, and short, twisting streets provide alternate paths for people to walk.

Socially, these neighborhoods are replete with cross-cutting ties. A resident going on vacation leaves a key with a small shop owner, or when a man seems to be threatening a child (who in Jacobs's illustration turns out to be a father chastising but not hurting his daughter), customers and residents who happen to be there peacefully gather around to ensure that nothing untoward happens. When a person stands at a bus stop on a Sunday, someone leans out the window to shout that the buses are not running. When inhabitants are away at work, people who work and shop in the neighborhood unselfconsciously keep watch, and at night when people are sleeping, customers in late night restaurants and bars—often "regulars" who have a stake in the welfare of the area—circulate and keep the streets secure. In the early evening, residents sit on stoops and keep the streets safe and alive. The welfare of those who live in the area depends on maintaining the goodwill of businesspeople and customers, and vice versa. Since interdependence cuts across interest groups, there are people awake and about at practically all hours of the day and night in sufficient numbers to help a spirit of accommodation and support prevail. There is no room for a gang or a clique to take possession of the neighborhood, and yet most people there belong to some identifiable group that restrains them from isolated acts of violence, predation, or destruction. It is only when one class of building or ownership or residents or entrepreneurs predominates over others that such a neighborhood begins to decline.

The impact of cross-cutting ties is corroborated by architect Patricia Brantingham and lawyer Paul Brantingham, who researched patterns of residential burglary in Tallahassee, Florida. Using any number of economic and demographic indices, they consistently find that burglary is lowest where adjoining city blocks are, on average, most alike, highest where blocks differ most. The only way to make burglary low throughout a city is to manage to have as much of the mix of people and wealth as possible contained within each and every city block. For example, the greater the spread of rents charged in each of two city blocks, the more likely that the average rent in one block will approximate the other; the more nearly each neighborhood approaches being a microcosm of the entire city, the harder it becomes to distinguish or discriminate among them. If so much variety is to be tolerated in a neighborhood, it will require that ties cut across many kinds of people who use the neighborhood, and that commonality of interest and interdependence among groups overwhelms the propensity of members of single groups to go it alone—either by taking over the neighborhood or by abandoning it.

There are obvious limits to variety that can be tolerated. Only the desperate will live or work or shop at the boundaries of a major airport, or at the gates of a smoke-producing oil refinery or steel plant. Only the wealthy can afford to live or have businesses where property taxes rise too high, or where a major department store pays high rent and is able to outsell all competitors in a neighborhood. Although there is room for some light industry, some exclusive shops, and for scattered high-rent residences, the general scale of enterprises in a heterogeneous neighborhood has to be small.

At a time when Adam Smith has gained renewed popularity among economists, it is interesting to note that his laissez-faire economy required that the average enterprise in most sectors be small. Monopolization of markets was anathema to Smith. One can easily suppose that he would have become an ally of the late economist E. F. Schumacher, who is perhaps best known for his book, *Small is Beautiful; Economics As If People Mattered.* Schumacher advocates the development of "appropriate technology" which would cost no more than five times the annual income of the lowest-paid worker who used it and would require creative input from each worker who used it. While technological ingenuity would be used to take the drudgery out of work, it would help industry remain labor intensive, requiring human labor rather than displacing it. Enterprises constructed around appropriate technology would be small, with a maximum of perhaps three hundred employees. Pay differentials in the enterprise could be tolerated, but would be restricted; workers would own the enterprise and, with representatives of community groups, sit on its board of directors. Part of the profits from the enterprise would go to the workers, part to community projects, and part to capital investment. An objective would be to have enterprises rely as heavily as possible on use of native and preferably renewable resources, and would concentrate sales as much as possible on local markets.

It is imperative that such a new economic model be followed. There is a worldwide depression because established economic bases are collapsing. World markets for finished products are nearly saturated despite the fact that a major portion of the world's work force does not actually produce. New industries, such as those in high technology, both promise to make more workers superfluous and have highly restricted markets. (The market for home computers and electronic games will only carry the sale of micro-chips so far.) Industries are borrowing more just to stay afloat while sales remain limited, and investment in plant and equipment continues to decline because there is little reason to expect expansion of consumption.

Centralized production is wasteful of finite natural resources, and heavy machinery produces intolerable pollution. As the energy demands of heavy industry become increasingly centralized, more intensive energy production is required, leading to technology such as building nuclear reactors, which is both inordinately expensive and extremely threatening to human and other life. The international interdependence of centralized production breeds such resentment and desperation during hard times that a world military holocaust looms larger. Meanwhile, the new conservative economics continues to limit investment to this losing economic cause and strangle the capacity of communities to build new economies to compensate.

The construction of new economies promises not only to contribute to peace with local communities, but to reduce the scale of and stake in international conflict. Appropriate technology does not make communities isolationist; indeed, it rests on a free exchange of information, people, and capital among communities. And as we have just seen, small-scale economies that foster cross-cutting ties actually blur community boundaries, so that it becomes less clear where one community ends and another begins. That each enterprise relies most on local resources, people, and sales scarcely implies that a business in one "locality" would compete in the exact same market as another close by. At its extreme, such an economy would entail a virtually seamless web of social, economic, and political networks around the globe.

137

But because networks are numerous and varied, and because their members are likely to have ties cutting across many networks, the consequences of economic failure of a single network would not be nearly so severe as they are when a large plant closes in a town today, neither for the members of the network themselves nor for others near or distant.

The development of such networks would increase the odds that every member of the community would be closely tied to several more. Membership in varied networks would offer a kind of freedom of movement and opportunity to those who could shift their involvement from one network toward another. The variety of allegiances would teach each community member to tolerate differences among people.

A key to establishing social peace is to offer people constructive outlets for energies that might otherwise be expended destructively. A tragic failing of conventional thinking about crime is its preoccupation with the negative: Crime hurts, so people must *not* do it. If crime is committed, the response is also negative: Let us drive the criminality out of the offender, or at least incapacitate the offender. By its preoccupation with repressing human behavior, conventional crime control consists of cures worse than the disease they are designed to attack.

If a society wants to stop people from committing crimes, it has to invest in things they *can* do instead. Human life consists of energy that craves outlet in interaction with others; the more constructive participation of people in community life can be expanded, the more social peace will reign.

In contemporary thought, childhood is the root of all human potential and of all evil. It is fair to say that childhood experience and its connection with delinquency has been the primary focus of American criminological research. Beyond criminology, Americans are also preoccupied with how children should be taught in school and raised at home. Just as criminal justice has swung back toward punishment, so American educators and parents have swung back toward the view that rigid discipline is needed to bring up children correctly. The idea that we ought to lay down strict rules for children, and that we ought to concentrate on having them perfect the rituals we call "basic skills," is a variant on the notion that law makes people behave.

Young children are notorious for energy, the epitome of life—with all its vices and virtues—as opposed to the quietude of death. A prominent response to this energy in recent years has been to diagnose it as hyperactivity, a form of learning disability, and tranquilize it out of existence.

This view of childhood—as a basically pathological condition—has blinded us to the rich constructive and creative potential that children offer to themselves and their communities. It is not merely that children cry for attention; their energy and involvement in activity intensifies when their work gains respect and appreciation from others. If children often need to be informed that their activity is obnoxious, they respond enthusiastically when discovering alternatives that please both adults and their peers. The greatest pleasure seems to come not by simply doing as told, but by having invented or initiated or created something that others appreciate. When a child who has spontaneously picked up a cloth and started to wipe furniture earns parental approval, it is almost magical to see the child so thoroughly enjoying "work." It is some time before the child learns that work done well has to earn a material reward.

Childhood ought to dispel notions that people are naturally lazy, that all work is drudgery, and that people

need a combination of coercion and bribery to be productive. Instead, apathy and laziness seem to be the learned
response of those who find that creative energy invariably
goes unappreciated, and concerted destructiveness shows
a combination of rage and the lack of alternatives for gaining recognition and attention. It is one thing to concede
adults the power to object to the intolerable and to demand what they deem necessary. It is harder to see objections and demands as the foundation of productive
childraising; the child who learns to be a creative con-
tributor to the welfare of others will do so only when
adults treat objections and demands as a necessary
nuisance, and appreciate creative efforts more.

What new kinds of investment are to establishing social
peace among adults, appreciation of creative and constructive activity is to bringing up productive and sane
children. At root, people behave best when we give them
opportunities to be valued for contributions they have a
hand in conceiving and initiating. When the child spontaneously wipes the furniture, it is partly our surprise at
seeing unexpected initiative from others that makes it
special. Law presumes that we know what we want from
others. If we succeed in achieving conformity in a changing world, we are apt to be disappointed by the sterility
and unhelpfulness of what we get. Children who have not
yet had ingenuity and initiative disciplined out of them
reveal that the best behavior we get is independent of law,
not caused by it.

Human Adaptability

A century ago, Charles Darwin gave us his provocative
and highly influential theory of natural selection or the
survival of the fittest. His theory soon became perverted

into a school of thought called "Social Darwinism." Social Darwinists hold that the people who have prospered more than others embody the traits that are genetically destined to rule and dominate the world. Whether we restrict breeding to the prosperous or try to coerce the poor into behaving like the prosperous, we are only promoting the survival of the fittest.

This flies in the face of Darwinist wisdom. Darwin noted that the characteristics that selected some species to dominate today's environment might predispose a species to extinction when the environment changes. For example, the size of dinosaurs predisposed them to dominate their environment when plant life and smaller animals that lived off of it thrived. It is now thought that the dust thrown up when one or more huge meteors crashed to earth so darkened the sky that much of the larger plant life died off, and that the dinosaurs' large appetites then proved their undoing. Darwin further held that future environmental contingencies were largely unforeseeable, as were mutations. Thus one could scarcely project which species would thrive tomorrow from knowing the condition of those of today.

Darwin went further. One could loosely predict which species were more likely than others to survive come what may, or which isolated regions were less likely to become barren than others. Species or ecological systems were more likely to survive the future if they had a large variety of characteristics. If one set of characteristics or adaptations lost the environmental gamble, a diverse gene pool would be more likely to provide a life form to fill the void. The concern is familiar to agronomists, who have aimed to diversify hybrid crops they introduce into any economy, so that if a blight were to wipe out one hybrid, the entire agricultural system would not be destroyed.

Today the world's people are learning the problem of

having invested in rationalizing, systematizing, and centralizing so much of the human economy. When recession sets in in the United States, it pulls the whole world down. President Reagan has been blaming the rest of the world while the rest of the world blames America. If, on the other hand, our enterprises had generally been small, using local materials and selling locally, then (a) failure in one economy would not so easily have caused failure in others, and (b) healthier enterprises in neighboring economies could have spawned replacements for the failures. So it is with armed conflict. The more rigidly the world is arrayed around a two-power axis, the more general the threat of annihilation. The more decentralized the management of conflict and the economic and political systems on which conflict is founded, the more limited the consequences of war among any pair of communities. For the sake of human prosperity and ultimately for the sake of human survival, Darwinian theory implies that new economies ought to be built around Schumacher's appropriate technology.

Within communities, Darwinian theory provides an explanation of why cross-cutting ties promote social peace. Conflict cannot be too highly organized, cannot be carried too far, because the variety of human adaptation to the environment, the variety of interest groups that intermingle, overwhelm any particular form that conflict takes. It is not law, but engineering and tolerating diversity of economic, social, and political arrangements, of organizations and enterprises in each of our communities, that makes people behave civilly toward each other.

BEYOND MYTH

Civil government, so far as it is instituted for the security of property, is in reality instituted for the defense of the rich against the poor.

Adam Smith, 1776

A PERSISTENT MYTH throughout history—one that seems to perpetuate itself in society after society, no matter how often proved wrong and no matter at what cost— is that a populace can be forced to behave as rulers see fit. The Romans felt that destroying Jesus would end the flow of his ideas. Members of the Spanish Inquisition felt they could force people to accept Catholicism. England sent troops thinking it could force the American colonists to obey the king's laws. Nazi Germany believed it could force others to do Hitler's bidding by killing off the dissidents. The United States fought a war in a vain effort to force the Vietnamese to accept what it thought was a proper government. Now there is El Salvador.

Most of the myths that dominate our policies on crime can be subsumed under this same dangerous notion—that people can be made to behave the way a superior armed authority would have them behave. It is time we freed ourselves of these myths.

143

There is no reason for us to remain tied to the fallacy that we can do nothing about crime. True, we may be able to do nothing about crime under current practices, but neither do we have to accept the myth that we could do any better under other economic systems. (Marxists who urge revolution as a way of ending crime only replace one myth with another.) Here follow some ideas that may help us move beyond myth.

Changes in Criminal Justice

On the bright side, Americans have long lived with rampant crime, in many periods without undue fear, in relative health and prosperity. Even now, our life expectancy is longer than ever; we will all die of course, but almost all of us will die of natural causes, not at the hands of another. Although we may constantly be suffering loss from theft and crime, perhaps when we visit the doctor, or take the car in for repairs, buy misrepresented products, or lose a purse at work, most of us still live pretty well, absorb the losses, and if we are aware of them, usually suffer more annoyance than lingering hardship.

We can take further comfort from the evidence that our risk of crime today is no worse than in those golden days of safety about which we reminisce. Moving beyond the myth of increasing crime also enables us to put the stories of brutality that dominate the news into perspective. In truth, the kinds of brutal crimes we most fear are rare events; except for isolated urban neighborhoods whose reputations for violence and decay are well deserved, we can still walk the streets in the safety to which we used to be accustomed. Indeed, freedom from irrational, excessive fear is the best defense against street crime, for it is well established that risk of street crime decreases as people circulate, interact, and observe each other more freely.

Switzerland is a model we might well follow. On the other hand, as American sociologist Marshall Clinard has reported, the Swiss consider themselves safe and secure, and do not spend much effort trying to bring offenders to task. Swiss police almost always issue summonses to court rather than arrest those they refer for prosecution. Prosecutors exercise wide discretion to settle crimes informally and to dismiss charges against those brought in by the people. The few defendants who end up in court are as often middle class as poor, and upon conviction, fines and suspended sentences are more common than imprisonment. There is no such thing as probation for those whose sentences are suspended; the Swiss consider special community supervision to be too wasteful with. Either the defendants get back into trouble with police, in which case they may end up in prison, or their sentences expire quietly. All told, the Swiss incarcerate only one-tenth as much of their populace as Americans do, and sentences very seldom last as long as one year. In prison, inmates are put to work in gainful occupations or relaxed to work outside prison. The Swiss do not bother with treatment or therapy, which they figure will do more to mess up the minds of offenders than reform them.

Moving beyond myth by no means implies eliminating police or prisons. Some people—notably the few who have repeatedly assaulted and killed with brutal disregard for human life—need to be safely isolated. A state that stands for the sanctity of life will confine such people as humanely, but securely, as possible, and will be able to do so more safely and reliably if prison overcrowding and bureaucratization are relieved by releasing the majority of inmates—who present little threat to society.

As to police, we need a responsive force upon whom

to call in times of trouble. It is consistently estimated that four out of five calls for assistance to police involve non-criminal matters. Even when law enforcement is not at issue, the police can provide much needed service: mediating between squabbling neighbors, calming a frightened and lonely person, finding a lost child, helping a derelict to shelter on a cold night. And of course, rare though the occasions might be, no one would deny the value of a quick police response to help someone who is being beaten or who has detected a prowler in the house. The skill and tempered use of force by police justify respect and support. Through changes in police training and reward structures, gentleness and social sensitivity can be given the priority they deserve over marksmanship and force. The Japanese police (black belts in martial arts though they all are) are a model of this kind of policing, as indeed are police in many affluent American communities. It is the style of the policing of our streets that needs changing, not the presence. One step in this process would be to end the police practice of counting offense reports and displaying them to the public. Indeed, where offenses are trivial enough, or where there is clearly insufficient evidence to pursue investigation and prosecution, there is no good reason to report offenses at all, let alone to publicize them.

A number of steps could be taken to encourage our criminal-justice officials to limit the force they use to deal with some crime. One big step, often suggested but seldom heard, would be to decriminalize vices like opiate use and prostitution. As we have noted, drug enforcement is the kind of practice that drives up the price of addiction and creates the chance that a product like heroin may be made life threatening when illicitly adulterated. Were opiate addicts given a safe and pure drug at minimal cost, the need to support an expensive habit would no longer drive them

146

to crime, and we would see an end both to the violence that surrounds illicit heroin distribution and the corruption of law enforcement that inevitably occurs in a hopeless war on addicts and low-level pushers. Similarly, if we decriminalized prostitution, women would have legal recourse against pimps and clients who brutalize them into submission, and the clients who seek them out would have recourse against robbery and theft.

At another level, even the most conservative elected officials are beginning to recognize how excessive a drain on tax money overuse of prisons is. Rather than asking our prosecutors and judges to justify "lenience" toward offenders, we might more rationally ask them to justify the expense of adding treatment programs and prison terms to criminal sentences. We ought to ask them to use court records to demonstrate that diversionary programs like the Victim Offender Reconciliation Program, are truly diverting offender from jail and prison. The Swiss are quite reasonable about rejecting treatment programs and years of prison and detention pending trial without demonstrable payoff. It is something of a mystery how tax-conscious Americans tolerate such freewheeling spending to accomplish so little with growing numbers of relatively minor offenders.

Should Government Invest in the American Economy?

Americans are known for wanting to keep government small, and, indeed, by Western standards Americans' tax burden is small. And yet in two important ways Americans depart from this belief, investing $100 per year per American in government funding of police and corrections and more than $1000 per year per American for military defense, with virtually no return in security or in help to victims. Moreover, because of the tax breaks given wealthy people and private corporations, the overall tax burden is unevenly distributed. Thus, also by Western standards, lower and middle income people in the United States pay a proportionately larger share of the expenses of government.

Some subsidies are hard to measure in money. Adam Smith decried the earliest major subsidy of big business: the corporate charter. Incorporation allows investors to hold themselves personally immune from liability for the acts of the business they create. This state guarantee of limited responsibility enables those with enough wealth to pool some of their capital with others they scarcely know or trust, to be managed by strangers who may have no investment at stake, on the chance that the pool of capital will be big and powerful enough to gain monopoly control of a market. Smith foresaw that the "invisible hand" of competition would make producers responsive to consumers' needs only where the threat of personal liability forced entrepreneurs to keep their businesses small.

Implicitly, too, Smith foresaw the emerging dangers of a professional class of managers of large corporations. It is common for chief executive officers today to enter their jobs under the premise that their tenure will be shortlived. They demand high bonuses based on short-term profit gains, and keep the long-term well-being of the business and the people it serves out of their calculations, plans, and thoughts. Managers and shareholders stand to get rich if they take their profits and then quit or divest, leaving the business to die of obsolescence and the company workers to look for new jobs. Those who take profits can and do reinvest abroad, and abandon American plants and jobs. As the rich get richer at taxpayers' expense, lower income workers are told that it is they who have to sacrifice wages if they are to compete to earn a livelihood.

Government subsidy of wealth is now referred to as supply-side economics. Supply-side economics means that the richer you are, the more the government spends to subsidize your freedom to pursue profit, or to borrow the title of Jeffrey Reiman's book, *The Rich Get Richer While the Poor Get Prison*. The contemporary version of "free enterprise" means that the wealthy are given a monopoly to profit at the expense of fellow citizens.

From tax law to laws of incorporation to administrative regulation to central banking to the criminalization of the underclass, American government is heavily involved in economic regulation and control. The distinction between so-called capitalist and socialist economies is not all that large: one system confers power and privilege on people called "the Fortune 500," while the other confers it on people called "leading Party members"; the inequities and waste of human potential is as debilitating to both kinds of societies.

So, advocating government investment in American enterprise is not saying that government get into a field that it has heretofore stayed out of. Instead, government should change its pattern of investment—away from protection of wealthy vested interests, toward increasing the security and welfare of the general populace. It is a lesser sin for American government to invest in creating jobs than for government to invest in destroying them, as it does now.

Proposals for Reinvestment

A basic precept of all religions from Buddhism to Puritanism makes common sense: socially meaningful

149

work is the heart of spiritual and secular well-being. Opportunity to do work that others appreciate—whether appreciation is shown as repayment of favors or in paying for food and shelter—is the social control measure best suited to making people behave civilly toward one another. Creation of meaningful, responsible jobs is the single most important contribution American government can make to domestic peace and security. For all the same reasons that imprisonment has failed to contain crime, empowering people to be paid and held accountable for work, stands to alleviate the problem.

The jobs that need creating can be divided into three categories: (1) businesses in which the general populace can produce goods and services, (2) businesses in which offenders can redeem themselves through legitimate production, and (3) structures in which criminal-justice officials can build ways of keeping peace in their communities without law enforcement.

A basic principle of engineering economic development can be derived from Adam Smith and Charles Darwin. Smith argued that enterprises had to be small, personalized, and adaptable to the free market; Darwin argues that the market (or environment) for supporting a species' life was essentially unpredictable. The gene pool that favored survival today might preclude survival under tomorrow's conditions. The species with the best prognosis for survival was the one in which the gene pool most varied, where some members would be most likely to be predisposed to get food and shelter under any circumstances.

The social corollary of Darwin is that demand for goods and services, and the capacity of producers to meet demand, is in large part luck. The fallibility of economic forecasts and unanticipated rises and falls in job markets reflect the fortuitousness of economic development. Production systems are the equivalent of gene pools. If an entire town depends for its livelihood on an auto plant, if auto sales fall off and the plant closes, the survival of the entire town is in jeopardy and the task of retooling a plant for thousands of workers is overwhelming. On the other hand, if the local economy is mixed, if farmers and tradespeople employ most of the residents, a failure of production of any single product affects fewer people, who can then either retool their production or move—as through kinship networks—to other enterprises whose products are selling.

The more evenly distributed a gene pool is, the more likely a species (or a society) will survive. Under the same principle, distributing idiosyncratic enterprises through the society—indeed throughout an international economy—is more important than deciding which products are to receive investment. It has been noted that the products in which the Japanese Ministry of International Trade and Industry has invested have not sold nearly so well, nor contributed to national income nearly so much, as products like cars that have received no subsidies and instead have emerged from systems of multiple producers (Japan has nine surviving major auto producers today). The Japanese economy is due for hard times; its production and marketing are too centralized, too internationalized, so that as Japanese labor becomes more expensive, Japanese business will inevitably suffer the fate of corporate America.

E. F. Schumacher's description of a successful British enterprise, the Scott Bader Commonwealth, highlights the features that Adam Smith's concept of small business needs to have. Producers of goods and services qualifying for major tax incentives, subsidies, low interest loans, loan guarantees, and market planning (those who would be generally subsidized by the government) would be chartered under the following conditions.

a) The company would have no more than several hundred workers (perhaps more in an economy on the American scale).
b) Workers would own shares of the corporation.
c) The people drawing most income would receive no more than (as in Scott Bader) seven times the income of the lowest paid worker.
d) The business would have a board of directors composed half of worker-owners (perhaps with one or more representatives of not-for-profit community groups to help tie the enterprise to its locale).
e) Much of the profits would be reinvested in the business, and half of the distributed profits would go to worker-owners, and half back into the community.

A demonstration that the enterprise was selling to or buying from local consumers or suppliers could qualify the producers for extra government support.

The government could also share information about the formation and success or failure of such enterprises, and push for development of Schumacher's "appropriate" technology: that which costs little, and can be employed on a small scale, and allows individual creativity to be put into work by removing the drudgery. The microcomputer is a contemporary example of appropriate technology in that it is inexpensive, can be introduced on a small scale, and requires individual creativity to shape its use to different needs.

The workers in Scott-Baderlike service organizations could receive broad insurance coverage for basic social services like medicine, law, child care, and psychotherapy. Full coverage would be reserved for citizens who invested in prepaid plans offered by qualifying organizations, small worker-owned cooperatives that contracted out extraordinary services like major surgery. These would be most likely to provide the greastest care at the lowest cost. For example, in a health maintenance organization in which secretaries, nurses, and paramedics were full partners with doctors, routine advice, diagnosis, and treatment could be provided under medical supervision without doctors having to see so many patients. In such a law firm, secretaries and clerks would ordinarily be well equipped to do such work as drafting simple wills and leases. Clients could even be trained by staff to do much of the simpler services for themselves, to become more self-reliant. When the size, distribution of profits, and ownership of service agencies are restricted, cost and service delivery become manageable.*

Investment in such agencies would create jobs and reduce the size of the underclass. Ownership of free means of production would give power to the chronically unemployed. It would not, however, prevent those underclass young men from remaining particularly vulnerable to imprisonment. The crime problem would stay with us. Two forms of direct action might alleviate this problem. One would be to make government service available to older adolescents who could choose where they served. They could, for instance, carry mail or work in veteran's hospitals or welfare offices or third-world villages. Universal services need not mean military service and need not be compulsary. Service as government workers would give the most vulnerable Americans some political protection from being picked up off the streets and dragged to jail, and would enable them to establish contacts and biographies as future applicants for private sector jobs.

The overabundance of people in prisons could be formed into inmate governments, much as Tom Murton (who in-

---

*There is a wealth of literature on and experience with worker cooperatives. Perhaps the most successful current American cooperatives are those for making plywood in Washington State. The foremost American authority on "worker self-managment" is Cornell University professor Jaroslav Vanek, author of several books on the subject. Perhaps the best analysis of the kind of worker ownership being proposed here is Robert Oakesnott's 1978 book, *The Case for Workers' Co-ops.*

spired Robert Redford's *Brubaker*) did in Arkansas. They could negotiate working and living conditions with prison staff subject to binding arbitration, much as collective bargaining works in the public sector. They could establish enterprises of the kind that qualified for government subsidy, perhaps invite families or friends to join them within the walls, and extend their communities beyond the walls for those who wanted to maintain their economic and social situation after release. In place of work release centers, offenders could be offered the option of setting up qualified worker-owned enterprises. Rehabilitation fails when it does not offer prisoners legitimate opportunity structures in "the free world." Rehabilitation that offers offenders a place to produce goods and services that communities need can succeed in reducing recidivism. The hope is that eventually prisons will not be used for offenders who can be rehabilitated, but only for a few intolerably dangerous people. Meanwhile, we are faced with the real problem of how to return inmates to society.

It would be a mistake, however, to reduce the numbers of first-time and repeat offenders without first finding new jobs for police, guards, and other criminal-justice officials. Threatening the jobs of these officials only makes them more desperate to arouse public fear of street crime and criminals by inflating crime figures, sending out special squads to make mass arrests, and chaining inmates to their bunks. Most police are already too well aware of how much spare time they have on their hands, and look hard for ways to justify their existence. To prevent officials from concentrating so hard on enforcing the law against underclass young men, we have to give them other jobs to do.

Collective bargaining between staff and inmates is a way of creating new jobs for prison officials. There are doubtless many things that inmates need done and that the staff would be willing to do which do not involve custody and security. In similar fashion, patrol officers and their superiors could negotiate priorities, standards, and performance evaluations of officials with residents of the communities they serve. The police, for their part, would be loath to violate the civil rights of outsiders or marginal residents of patrol districts. The residents should be able to imagine services they would appreciate which the police would never imagine providing. Job descriptions in which law enforcement became increasingly superfluous could evolve out of this structure.

At the federal levels, there are many forms of white-collar crime and official corruption upon which law enforcement could concentrate. Since so much criminal activity by the wealthy crosses communities, it would be appropriate for federal and state officials to concentrate on "respectable" crime and leave street crime to city and county officials. This would give the federal and state officials plenty to do, would attack the more serious part of the crime problem, would help counter the bias of law enforcement against the poor, and would retard the number of offenders sent into prison systems.

In sum, the key to governmental success in managing the crime problem is to invest in businesses and programs best suited to producing social peace and welfare in American communities.

Is Investment Worth the Risk?

Although small businesses are notorious for failing, they have been the source of 70 percent of the growth in American employment in the last decade. Were government prepared to reinvest in creating small-scale enterprises, it would have to be prepared for a number of failures and for slow progress toward full and secure employment overall. Social change entails risk.

This risk can be weighed against the proven failure of conventional approaches to investment and social control. Jobs are leaving the country, prisons are filling, fear of crime continues to mount, and the major part of the crime problem—crime at the top—continues to be virtually ignored. Here are two centuries of an approach to government investment that not only risks failure, but demonstrates failure through its growing capacity to generate social and economic decline. Progress through reinvestment may be slow and uncertain; progress through current government investment is virtually inconceivable.

Myths may be comforting. They may sustain the hope that threats to personal security are a limited problem that can be managed by whipping weaker members of society into shape. However attractive, the myths about crime have nevertheless proved themselves invalid; wars against crime based on the myths have never been won. It is high time we started being practical about dealing with crime, and to be practical, we have to move beyond myth.

156

EPILOGUE

How long, Your Honor, will it take for the world to get back the humane emotions that were slowly growing before the war? How long will it take the calloused hearts of men before the scars of hatred and cruelty will be removed?

...I need not tell you how many upright, honorable young boys have come into this court charged with murder, some saved and some sent to their death, boys who fought in this war and learned to place a cheap value on human life. You know it and I know it. These boys were brought up in it. The tales of death were in their homes, their playgrounds, their schools; they were in the newspapers that they read; it was the least sacred thing in existence and these boys were trained to this cruelty.

It will take fifty years to wipe it out of the human heart, if ever. I know this, that after the Civil War in 1865, crimes of this sort increased marvelously. No one needs to tell me that crime has no cause. It has as definite a cause as any other disease, and I know that out of the hatred and bitterness of the Civil War crime increased as America had never known it before. I know that growing out of the Napoleonic Wars there was an era of crime such as Europe had never seen before. I know that Europe is going through the same experience today; I know it has followed every war; and I know it has influenced these boys so that life was not the same to them as it would have been if the world had not been made red with blood.

Clarence Darrow
Leopold-Loeb trial, 1924

IN THE LATE 1950s we entered the Fourth American War on Crime. The war has not yet ended.

Each of our four wars on crime started as those who were children during a military war reached adulthood. After the War of 1812, after the Civil War, after World War I, and after World War II, a generation of veterans turned to war against its own offspring.

This Fourth War has been prolonged, perhaps because we moved from World War II to Korea to Vietnam with almost no respite.

We have seen that statistics in this war on crime do not indicate the true shape or size of theft, murder, and other unlawful behavior. The pattern by now is familiar. The Federal Bureau of Investigation released its figures for 1983 crime on a Friday (April 19, 1984) to give them big coverage on a slow news weekend. Around the country, we heard that "serious crime" had dropped 7 percent, a second straight year of decline, and we asked our police to tell us why. Predictably, the police said that the generation of postwar babies, *poor* postwar babies in particular, was growing too old to sustain its unlawfulness. The police said they were getting more dangerous offenders off the streets and into prisons. The police said that neighborhood crime watches were scaring offenders off.

Not so. When governments cut agency budgets, police morale suffers, and demoralized police are inclined to do two things. First, they slack off on paper work and responsiveness to complainants, so that offense reporting falls off. Second, they use campaigns of traffic and public-order enforcement to vent their frustrations, which lead to a lot of arrests, but not for the kinds of offenses the FBI records. The net result is that crime figures go down while the police feed more people into jail and prison. So the figures indicate that police tactics have changed, but not that people risk crime more or less. If the pattern runs true to form, we will see increasing reports of police corruption, as the police suffer the consequences of arresting or antagonizing the wrong people in their public-order crackdowns. Underneath these figures, we can expect greater police abuses of civil liberties, more police shootings, and the like.

To win a shooting war, a nation needs to identify a foreign army or government, isolate it, and force it to surrender. In a war on crime, we face no army or alien government. And when we try to isolate the enemy by identifying it as underclass young men, we put ourselves in the position of trying to beat our presumed opponent by taking only pawns. Even if the analogy held and chronically unemployed young men were "a dangerous class" of soldiers in crime, taking each to prison would still leave the more powerful enemy pieces—the white-collar criminals and institutional power brokers—on the board.

A prominent advocate of retributive punishment, Ernest Van den Haag, has put it this way: Most of the crime we have to fear is at least implicitly organized into markets—stolen goods and drugs, for example. When we imprison the pawns, the market merely pays the going price to recruit new soldiers. In fact, as the war drives soldiers' pay up, the market expands. This, as we have noted, is exactly what has happened to the markets for supplying marijuana and heroin, and these markets are undoubtedly representative of a general pattern. Whether or not Americans are hurt more by crime today than they have been for the past two centuries, forces of criminality have undoubtedly become more rather than less entrenched as the forces of criminal justice have waged their wars. Far from discouraging or displacing the kings and queens of American crime, the forces of law and order have served to enrich and secure their positions.

It is hard enough for citizens to separate friend from foe in any civil war. When the enemy is crime, and when most citizens know (as decades of self-report surveys indicate they do) that they themselves have periodically been publicly intoxicated, or have used illicit drugs, or have stolen or vandalized, or have assaulted others from time to time, confusion becomes complete. As increased investment in police and prisons yields no demonstrable progress toward defeating crime, frustration and fear grow, too. In the end, the forces of law and order victimize those they are hired to protect and defend.

This is the life Americans live with the myths that cause crime. A people who persist in fighting a myth-bound war on crime only defeat themselves. It is time Americans turned to making peace with themselves, and asked their government to invest in enterprises on which a peaceful social order can be built.

STUDY INDEX

166

and deterrence, 13, 129-130
effect on crime, 2-3
and "just deserts", 121, 159
and mediation, 93
and reformatories, 109-110
and retribution, 16, 125-126
in Sweden, 114-115, 117, 119
in Switzerland, 145

Crime

causes of, 9-10, 14
    economic, 10-12
    nature of American, 31-33
    poverty, American view of, 39, 42-45
    poverty, class bias, 43
    poverty, conventional view of, 36
    poverty, punishment of the poor, 38
    poverty, treatment of, 38
    poverty, and the urban poor, 37
cost of, 33
extent of, 9, 12, 21-22
fear of, 9, 11, 22, 25, 144, 160
measurement of, 22-30, 158
    and the "dark figure", 23
    and the Federal Bureau of Investigation (FBI),
        25-26, 28-29
    history of, 22-26
    and homicide, 29
    Indianapolis, IN, 27-29
    labeling (stigmatization), 84, 86
    "offenses known to the police", 25
    police control of, 24-29
    self-report studies, 34
    unfounding, 28
    Uniform Crime Report, 25-26
    victimization surveys, 29-30
solutions to, 2
    economic, 6, 136, 138, 140-142, 149-155
    environmental, 133-135
    Swiss model, 145